Picture my world

Photography in primary education

written by Kamina Walton

edited by Vivienne Reiss

curriculum adviser Kim Walden

THE ARTS COUNCIL OF ENGLAND

Contents

Contents

Foreword

Children read visual images before they are able to understand the written word. This gives the photographic image a significant but much under utilised role in education. In the late nineties, when we are experiencing a visual revolution in which an unprecedented amount of information is communicated visually, the use of images in teaching children demands much broader application. This book enables teachers to harness sill and digital imagery as a powerful tool to engage children creatively in subjects across the curriculum. By increasing their visual skills through a range of subject activities using photography, children also become better equipped to understand the many visual languages of art.

Marjorie Allthorpe-Guyton

Director of visual arts and architecture

The Arts Council of England

Welcome!

'Welcome to my amazing world!'[1]

We live in a visual world. Young children receive a great deal of information from visual sources and consequently they are intensely visually aware. For most children the act of looking comes before words, it is the primary learning experience. Children's television, games, books, videos and computer games all acknowledge and exploit children's ability to understand a range of complex visual languages.

Photography is one of the most powerful visual media which informs the way both young and old communicate; it is everywhere we look. We see photographs on advertising hoardings, in newspapers, and we carry photographs around with us and share them with our friends and families. We use photographs to communicate our ideas, to tell stories and to document occasions. Photography contributes substantially to the ways in which we understand ourselves, others and the world we live in. At a very young age children learn how to pose for the camera and are able to engage with photographs in an informed way.

The revised National Curriculum Orders include photography as one of the media for teaching art, and photographers have been added to the list of artists, crafts people and designers whose work can be introduced in the classroom. *Picture my world* proposes photography as an accessible tool of visual communication and of developing visual literacy. Not only is visual literacy one of the core objectives of the revised curriculum for art, it is an important concept which can underpin the delivery of the whole curriculum.

Picture my world demonstrates practical ways of using photography right across the primary curriculum. It brings together an exciting range of ideas, activities and images placing the child at the centre of her or his learning experience. Much of the work pushes the boundaries of the photographic medium itself, presenting photo-sculpture, drama-based shadow pictures, digital images and multimedia projects. It also explores basic darkroom techniques and a wealth of activities which look at non-darkroom based projects.

This book highlights the work of photographers, artists and those working in gallery and community education who, with teachers, have helped to develop innovative practice in schools. It celebrates the work from the Arts Council teacher advisory posts which were established through collaboration with LEAs. *Picture my world* points to a way of working which acknowledges the resources of local museums, libraries, arts centres and galleries. These organisations can support curriculum development through artists' residencies, practical workshops and interpretive materials.

To coincide with the publication of this book, the exhibition *The amazing me ... and other stories* has been launched at The Photographers' Gallery, London. It is the first large-scale national touring exhibition which presents a collection of photographic work from primary schools across the country and introduces the work from the new Arts Council photography teacher development posts in Manchester, Bristol and Middlesex/London.[2] Some of the work shown in *The amazing me* exhibition appears here in the context of its production. The book and exhibition have attracted wide press and media coverage. The creativity and imagination of the children involved has resulted in work which has engaged a diverse audience from the arts, entertainment and education.

Welcome!

While young children pose for a camera their engagement with the medium is usually fairly passive. The work in this book and exhibition turns the table and represents children as active and articulate makers and producers of photographs and images. It shows that children can make both eloquent and vivid images of real and imagined worlds.

The feeling of success and achievement are best described by William Goh, 'My friends liked my face in it. My family were proud of it and me and I was very pleased when I saw it on the wall in school.' William's photograph is shown here in the PSHE and RE chapter and has also been widely reproduced in the national press.

Both *Picture my world* and *The amazing me ... and other stories* are tributes to all those who have been involved in photography in education initiatives. The book and exhibition are part of the work of the visual arts and architecture department of the Arts Council which engages with formal education. This work in a classroom context, this has led to some of the most challenging and exciting ways of using photography in education.

We look to the children and young people whose work informs this book for a new generation of artists and audiences.

Vivienne Reiss

Visual arts officer

Arts Council of England

1. *The Telegraph Magazine.* 11 March 1995
2. The new posts replace teacher advisory posts and have been established through collaborations between higher education and the independent photography sector. They initiate practical school and community programmes, produce curriculum materials, work with initial teacher training and also deliver INSET (in-service educational training). They establish photography in education modules on ITT (initial teacher training), post-graduate and MA courses. The posts also look at research and development, exploring ideas which relate to photography in education and to the understanding of contemporary visual arts, within a wider visual culture. This work is disseminated through the production of publications and through conferences and events.

Introduction

Picture my world is a compendium of successful classroom initiatives that have come out of research into uses of photography in primary education over recent years. It bears witness to the enthusiasm and hard work of teachers, photographers and people working in gallery and community education whose ideas and inventions are described within its pages. But it is no coincidence that these initiatives have taken place. This introductory account is intended to place these practices into context. First by charting how photography has been used in primary education and the factors that have shaped its development, and second by setting out some of the book's guiding principles for using photography across the curriculum.

The history of photography in education

There is nothing new about photography in schools. For a long time cameras have been used for recording the highlights of school life and are considered part of a school's media resources. Photography has been used in education too. It has also provided a hands-on way to demonstrate basic scientific ideas – bringing together the two key areas of optics and light through the construction of pinhole cameras. Making images with light-sensitive materials has been a popular art activity too – even the very youngest child can create sun pictures and light drawings.[1] Early uses of photography in education have often concentrated on the practicalities of making pictures rather than the meaning of pictures and this emphasis limited its impact in primary schools. However, since the 1970s there has been a growing interest in photography as a form of communication in its own right.

Media education

Since the 1970s primary school specialists were becoming more aware of the influence of the media on the lives of small children. Studies indicated that children were getting much of their information about the world from media sources, yet schools were equipping children with the necessary skills to learn from traditional print sources, such as books, but ignoring or even denigrating children's experience of the broader media which was considered irrelevant to education.[2] There were debates about whether teachers should be teaching about the media rather than just using media as a teaching aid. Teachers started to develop media education in schools using the user-friendly technologies of video and high street film processing and printing.

Photography is generally considered to be a good starting point for media education as it is the most accessible and technically straightforward medium.[3] It was proposed that 'media literacy' could be developed from nursery age onwards starting from the premise that a picture is a 'text' to be 'read' much like any other form of print. Media education advocated examining photographs by identifying all the elements within the picture's frame and scrutinising them for their meanings. Reading pictures could be undertaken alongside conventional literacy development from the earliest years and photography was seen as a first stepping stone on the route to studying time-based media such as film and television.

The Arts Council and the Regional Arts Associations

At the same time the Arts Council and the Regional Arts Associations were starting to consider how best they could collaborate with the education sector to increase access to the arts. After

all, today's schoolchildren are tomorrow's artists and audiences. The first joint venture funding schemes enabled artists to undertake fellowships and residencies within educational establishments. Later, artists in schools schemes provided an opportunity to develop more practical and specific inputs for both teachers and their pupils through artists' residencies, teachers' workshops, educational publications and touring exhibitions. These interventions broke new ground but they were often short-lived and so their impact on the development of photography in the curriculum was inevitably limited.

Perhaps of longer term significance was the development of educational activities based in photography centres and galleries. Education posts were established in some organisations with the intention of providing interpretative programmes, guided exhibition tours, teachers' workshops and teaching materials as a service to schools and colleges. In other areas outreach programmes placed photography in community arts contexts. These strategies enabled organisations to develop longer term links with teachers, schools and Local Education Authorities (LEAs) and to become known locally for their specialist skills, knowledge and facilities. Indeed, there were a handful of community photography projects which were developing ways of using photography specifically with young children.

Community photography

Among these were Mount Pleasant Photography Workshop in Southampton and Blackfriars Photography Project in south London. Both projects evolved approaches to photography which recognised that, while children could gain a great deal from learning basic camera skills, the strength of photography as an educational tool was that it provided children with a means of expression. Cameras could give children a 'voice' through which to communicate and make sense of their experience at home, in the community and at school. Opportunities were created to work in partnership with schools over extended periods of time. These initiatives pointed to the potential of photography in schools and, through their strong multi-cultural ethos demonstrated how photography could assist in making the curriculum relevant to the needs of these children.

Interest in photography grew but it still held only a marginal role in the school curriculum. The division between theory-led approaches in media education and English and the practical picture-making activities used within art, meant that there was no coherent approach to photography in schools. Within LEA structures photography was subsumed under either art or media education in English but lacked any firm base within the authorities.

Advisory teachers in photography

In order to inject new impetus into the development of photography in education, the Arts Council set in train a process of research and development, collaborating for the first time with local education authorities. Over a period of five years, six teacher advisory posts were set up in joint funding initiatives with local education authorities with the intention of bringing together the interests of photography in education to develop coherent models of classroom practice and county-wide INSET programmes.[4] These advisory teachers drew on the innovative practices of the independent photography sector, collaborating with photographers, community arts agencies and galleries to develop ways of working in the classroom and some of that work is documented in this book.

Education reform

However, these initiatives were overtaken by the fundamental reorganisation of education which resulted from the Education Reform Act 1988. These measures meant that the management of schools passed from LEAs to the governors of individual schools and introduced the National Curriculum. When the consultative working parties were set up to

draft a National Curriculum submissions were invited from interested parties. This provided a unique and timely opportunity for the Arts Council to influence the shape of the National Curriculum. The Photography in Education Working Party was set up by the Arts Council to draw together representations from those with an interest in photography in education. Papers were compiled for working parties in various subjects, including art. When the statutory Orders were duly issued in 1992, they confirmed that photography had been assimilated into the new curriculum for art.

Creating vision: Photography in the National Curriculum

At the same time the the Photography in Education Working Party began working on the book *Creating Vision: Photography in the National Curriculum* which was published in 1994 by the Arts Council of Great Britain. This book proposed an approach to photography which integrated the theoretical and practical aspects of photography education with media education. It advocated a place for photography within the National Curriculum by drawing up its own attainment targets and matrix of how photography might be taught throughout the Key Stages. *Creating Vision* was the first attempt to provide a complete theoretical overview of the educational potential of the subject and to map out a curriculum for photography. The book also set out ways in which photography could be involved more actively in delivering the subjects of the National Curriculum.

Photography in education now

The Final Orders 1995

In recognition that the original Orders were overloaded, Education Secretary, John Patten commissioned their revision in 1994. Early consultation drafts erased photography from the art curriculum. However, this was resisted with representations from the arts sector, including the Arts Council, and the final Orders reinstated photography at all three Key Stages. This has been a significant step for the development of photography. It is now one of the recognised media for teaching art and photographers have been added to the list of artists, crafts people and designers whose work can be introduced into the classroom.

However, reference points in the Orders do not in themselves facilitate classroom practice. Many teachers feel poorly equipped to teach some areas of the art curriculum, both in terms of their own training and the lack of resources. Moreover, the new slimmed-down Orders give no practical guidance to teachers.

Picture my world: photography in primary education

Our aim is that *Picture my world* should meet this need by bringing together tried and tested examples of classroom practice in one book. Many of the ideas described here are the result of collaborations between advisory teachers, photographers, artists and gallery education staff working in schools and pooling their professional skills. There are a number of projects undertaken in schools attended by children with special educational needs and the resulting work demonstrates a range of interesting and innovative approaches.

Some of the classroom practices have been related to exhibitions at local galleries close to schools. Photography exhibitions can be found in all kinds of different places including museums, libraries and arts centres. These organisations play an important role in resourcing the development of photography in education. Local galleries offer support for curriculum development by organising artists' residencies, practical workshops, technical advice, follow-up visits and, perhaps most usefully, publishing teachers' packs for little or no cost.

Introduction

Child-centred

Picture my world starts from the premise that the child should be placed at the centre of her or his own learning experience. To do this the book has distilled the curriculum down to a set of simple questions which each subject seeks to answer: In the art chapter the question is – How do I see it? In PSHE and RE – Who am I? In geography – Where do I live? In history – How did I live? In science – How do I understand the world? In English – How do I tell it? Then it sets about showing different ways in which photography can be used to answer these questions.

Teacher-friendly approach

In order to help teachers who may have felt reticence in using photography in the past because they have felt it was either too technical or specialised, the book takes a straightforward teacher-friendly approach. It seeks to demystify photography through the use of jargon-free language as much as possible and there is a section containing technical tips to meet teachers' practical needs. The book is organised on a subject-by-subject basis but it sets out ways of meeting the subject requirements through cross-curricular approaches. Most of the projects are designed to deliver a number of subjects within the National Curriculum.

Each chapter covers a subject and is colour-coded. The subjects are cross-referenced with one another with the help of colour-coded icons running down the side of the text next to relevant activities. In addition there are planning grids at the end of each chapter which reference subject attainment targets and programmes of study. We have chosen to highlight particular reference points in the Orders but individual teachers will no doubt make other connections within the curriculum.

One of the most common concerns voiced by teachers about using photography in the classroom is the cost. However, the reader will discover on looking through the practical exercises documented in this book that there are many ways of keeping the costs low. By the same token, not all photography activities require a camera. Children can use 'found' photos from sources such as newspapers, magazines, photopacks and so on. These found pictures can be cut up, collaged, copied and drawn on. The principle remains the same: making pictures opens the door to learning how photographs can be understood.

Classroom practice

This book is not intended to be prescriptive or even comprehensive. *Picture my world* offers up a work-in-progress model of photography in education. We hope readers will try out some of these ideas, add to them, alter them and build new versions to suit their particular circumstances. Deliberately, the framework does not use academic research procedures. It was written from within the classroom and so accounts are given in the form of lesson plans gathered from the experience of teachers and practitioners working in different kinds of schools. It tries to give some sense of what it feels like for both the teacher and the child to be doing these activities in the classroom.

This book is picture-led. Most of the photographs were made or directed by children and they are the subject of many of their pictures. These images provide a vivid insight into the children's minds, their sense of themselves, their ideas and their ways of seeing the world. It is the children's work, more than any number of words, which demonstrates how photography can make a contribution to the primary curriculum.

A new agenda

By drawing together new classroom practices *Picture my world* is seeking to map out a new agenda for photography in primary education. For many teachers photography in education has meant the practical activity of making and printing pictures in the darkroom. This book hopes to broaden the definition to include learning about how photographs communicate through photographic (visual) language and photographic cultural forms. The new definition of photography in education centres around the concept of *visual literacy* which is one of the core objectives of the revised curriculum for art. We live in a world that communicates through the visual media and visual literacy is crucial to understanding them.

What is visual literacy?

The familiarity and realism of the photograph can help children relate their own experience to the subjects of the curriculum. The American writer and critic Susan Sontag once wrote that 'photographed images do not seem to be statements about the world so much as pieces of it ...'[5] Because photographs very often look like the things they refer to we often assume that they make sense all on their own and that there is nothing to learn but this is not the case.

All visual media have their own language through which they communicate their meaning. Whether we are looking at a sculpture, computer animation, painting or photograph, each form has its own characteristics which we can learn to 'read' in the sense we read the picture's subject. These aesthetic considerations may include uses of colour, pattern, texture, shape, space, framing and composition which are commonly understood as the language of art.

Content

To start to understand how these considerations relate to the content of the picture and how they affect its meaning, we can ask simple questions about the choices taken when it is made: for example we might ask why a photographer has chosen to use black and white film rather than colour? Where do we see black and white photographs? Where do we usually see colour photographs? It is important to bear in mind that most visual images are the result of selections like this. The factors that shape the picture can be explored by children through a number of practical activities described in the chapter on art. Indeed these activities to develop visual literacy skills inform all the other projects in the book and so each project is cross-referenced back to art.

When taking, developing and printing a picture, a series of technical decisions are made which will shape its meaning too. These decisions will include lighting, camera angle, distance from the subject, print size and so forth, which we read also recognising, for example, that blur means movement. However, it should be remembered that the aesthetic and technical possibilities are not the only factors which influence how we understand a picture.

Conventions

Very often photographs will conform to certain conventions. For example, family albums will be full of photographs of colour snaps of beaming babies rather than black and white pictures of tear-stained toddlers. In turn these conventions are reproduced, re-fashioned, parodied and inverted by advertising and the whole range of popular media until these visual conventions become visual clichés – a kind of visual shorthand which we all recognise and use. It is important to remember that we draw not only on our knowledge of the subject in the picture but other photographs, visual arts, personal experiences and viewpoints too.

Context

The process of production and circulation of photographs influences the way a picture communicates its meaning. Teachers will know themselves from using word processors in the classroom that type is different from hand-writing, not just in terms of accessibility but also in intention and status. Presentation shapes the message. The placing of the same photograph in different situations – on the front page of a newspaper, in a family album or on a giant advertising billboard illustrates how the meaning is altered by the context in which it is seen.

Introduction

Visual education

Visual literacy is not just about being able to read and recover meaning from photographs, it is also about being able to construct them. Who would teach a child how to read but not write? To be fully literate children must also be able to express themselves visually and to make the media their own, children can become remarkably articulate with a camera, as we can see from the work in this book, not by just making a record but by actually expressing a point of view. Photography is an excellent media for practical work with children as it is easy to learn and the right scale for small hands.

Visual literacy is about the relationship between investigating and making visual forms and the knowledge and understanding of the different ways in which they communicate meaning in the art curriculum. Because so much of the curriculum is delivered through visual images at Key Stages 1 and 2, skills in visual literacy are vitally important – they can underpin the delivery of the whole curriculum. It is hoped that *Picture my world* can contribute to a broadening of the role of visual education and to the redefinition of photography within primary education.

Looking forward

Visual literacy is becoming more significant now that we are undergoing an 'information revolution'. If the Internet, cable and satellite TV and other technologies prove to be even half as important as they are predicted to be, there will be a shift away from the primacy of the printed word in favour of 'new literacies'. The new technologies are bringing about a process of convergence within media production which will mean that children will become adept at interpreting not just written text but pictures and sound too. The multimedia PC is starting to make its way into schools. If, as the current Education Secretary Gillian Shepherd suggested, the revised Orders are to take us into the 21st century, then the curriculum must equip our children to live in a changing world. For this reason, the teaching of visual literacy must be seen as important as other literacies in the primary curriculum.

Kim Walden

Notes and references

1. These different ways of using photographic materials were best articulated in the Ilford Photography Research Project and results were published in a manual *Classroom Photography* (Ilford, 1984)
2. *A Language for Life (The Bullock Report)* (HMSO, 1975). In chapter 2 Bullock gives the average figure of 25 hours of television viewing each week for pupils aged five to fourteen.
3. See Andrew Bethell's teaching books *Eyeopeners* (CUP, 1981).
4. The participating counties were Hertfordshire, Somerset, Cheshire, Yorkshire, Sussex and Northumberland.
5. See Susan Sontag's *On Photography*. Penguin. ISBN 0 140053972

How do I see?

Art

How do we see?

How do I see?

The purpose of art within the curriculum is to develop children's visual literacy skills, to encourage self-expression and creativity, to develop creative and practical skills, and to introduce the work of other artists. This chapter is central to the book and aims to redefine the position of photography within art. It offers a starting point for using photography as a tool for learning right across the curriculum.

Photography is the most popular picture-making activity in the UK. In the past it has been seen as a practice that requires the acquisition of technical skills with the focus on darkroom-based work. However, as this book demonstrates, the definition of photography within art, and within education in general, has broadened to include a whole range of non-darkroom based practices, digital technologies, and the use of found images. The medium is also ideally suited to teaching children about visual literacy, in other words, the ways in which meaning is created within visual images. By teaching children to 'read' images not only will their ability to communicate through their own images develop but they will have a far greater understanding of the visual world around them.

Photographic images surround us and are part of our everyday lives. Photography is therefore an important practice and can be an accessible means of introduction to the study of other artists' work. One exciting and effective way of introducing new practice into the classroom is to invite photographers into school as photographers or artists in residence. Photography as an artistic practice has now been added to the range of work of artists, craftspeople and designers that children should study at all three Key Stages. By having a photographer working in the classroom not only are children given the opportunity to study that photographer's work and their approach firsthand, but it serves as a reference point and source of inspiration for the children's own work. At the same time teachers who may feel the need for fresh ideas and expertise can gain stimulus from the experience.

To fulfil the curriculum requirements for art, teachers can draw on the resources and expertise of local galleries, arts organisations, community arts groups and local artists. This is also a good way of accessing contemporary work, a particular requirement of the art curriculum, as local galleries and arts centres frequently show the work of practising local or regional artists. Many of these organisations offer training through workshops and short courses and may also run arts activities for children linked directly with touring or gallery-based exhibitions, or have teachers' packs available that can provide a focus for cross-curricular topic work. ■

Aims

- To develop children's skills in visual literacy, thus enabling them to 'read' visual images and control visual meaning within their own work, leading to an understanding of the visual world around them.
- To enable children to express themselves effectively through a visual medium.
- To use photography as a tool for gathering information, improving powers of observation and skills in interpretation.
- To highlight the place of other photographers' work and show its potential as reference material and as a source of inspiration for the children's own work.
- To give children appropriate opportunities to develop and apply an information technology capability to the study of art.

How do I look?

Before children begin to use a camera in the classroom they should be taught how to look carefully through a viewfinder. One of the most important starting points is to teach a child to look through their viewfinder with one eye closed so that they can frame their image successfully, and experience how vision is affected by seeing through one eye as opposed to two. Many children find this difficult as it is not a physical action they are used to, but they can practise by looking through a variety of monocular devices found around the classroom, such as telescopes and toilet rolls, covering one eye with their hand, or asking another child to cover it for them. Alternatively, an eye patch could be made from paper or material that covers one eye, achieving the same result. ■

'Framing'

The framing activity has been used as a starting point for nearly all the projects outlined in this book. The images overleaf were produced by a child at Barton Hill Junior School, Bristol.[1]

By giving a child a viewfinder you are also helping to structure the way in which they look at the world around them, thus developing their visual perception. Once they have got used to looking with only one eye you can give them smaller rectangular viewfinders, similar to a camera's. When looking through the viewfinder the children should be encouraged to think about whether their subject is best framed by holding the viewfinder horizontally or vertically, what is included and excluded in the frame, and to experiment by moving closer and then further away from their subject to see how it increases or decreases in size. ■

'Framing' activities

- Give each child a plastic slide mount or similar sized cardboard frame and ask them to walk around the classroom looking through it with one eye closed, as though they were looking through a camera's viewfinder. Make sure they hold it approximately 3–5cm in front of their eye so that it successfully frames what they see.
- Encourage the children to explore what happens when they move closer to something or further away, and to see how the framing varies depending on whether they hold the viewfinder horizontally or vertically.

- When they have found an area that interests them (not including other children as they will move) give each child a piece of drawing paper and ask them to draw a rectangle approximately the same size as a standard colour print. This will be the picture space where they will draw what they can see through their viewfinder.
- When the children are drawing encourage them to keep looking through the frame so that their vision has boundaries, and to fill the rectangle on their paper, concentrating more on shapes than detail. They should understand that objects do not float in space and therefore they should draw everything they see. Whether they have chosen to use their viewfinder vertically or horizontally they should do their drawing the corresponding way.

Barton Hill Junior School

Barton Hill Junior School

- Once the drawing is finished ask them to take a photograph that looks as much like their drawing as possible, again considering whether they need to hold the camera horizontally or vertically.
- When the film has been processed ask the children to compare their photographs with their drawings, looking for similarities and differences, and to write about their observations. ■

Resources

- Plastic slide mounts (or small cardboard frames)
- Drawing paper and pencils
- Clip boards
- 35mm camera and colour print film

'Animals'

Any photograph we take will be affected by a number of choices that are made before pressing the shutter. Children need to be taught how to make these choices in relation to framing, camera angle, distance and viewpoint to be able to control the picture-making process.

A small primary school in the village of Compton, West Sussex, was invited to take part in a photographic initiative, working with a

photographer commissioned by South East Arts, on a project that aimed to create interest and awareness of photography amongst children and staff throughout the school.[2] The project involved investigating life from an animal's point of view which proved to be an excellent way of developing the children's understanding of viewpoint, angle, distance and composition. ■

'Animals' activities

- Collect together a range of snapshots that show examples of photographs that have 'gone wrong'. These could include heads or feet that have been chopped off, poor focus caused by the subject or camera moving, or by the photographer getting too close to the subject, tilted horizon, or fingers over the lens. Ask the children to identify the cause of these mistakes and to suggest ways that they might be avoided – if they have already tried the framing exercise they should find it easy to provide the answers.
- At Compton the children then used a still video camera connected to a television monitor to experiment with framing, camera angle, distance and viewpoint. They were asked to make deliberate mistakes, such as those described above, and then to correct them. In this way when one child moved the camera the whole class could immediately see the effects created on the monitor. If you do not have access to a video camera you could ask the children to describe what they are seeing through the viewfinder and the changes they see when they move around.
- Using the example of animals divide the class into groups and ask each group to choose an animal they would like to represent. They can then pretend to be that animal, pretend to react to it, or experiment with both points of view. In this way the camera will become the animal's or the observer's eyes, encouraging imaginative exploration of the children's surroundings.
- When mounting the resulting photographs the children could create captions for them and include photocopies of their chosen animal from books or magazines to make the animal's viewpoint clear. ■

Resources

- 35mm camera and colour print film
- Video camera and monitor (if available)
- Ladder, or other means of looking down on their subject
- Images of chosen animals to use in the final display

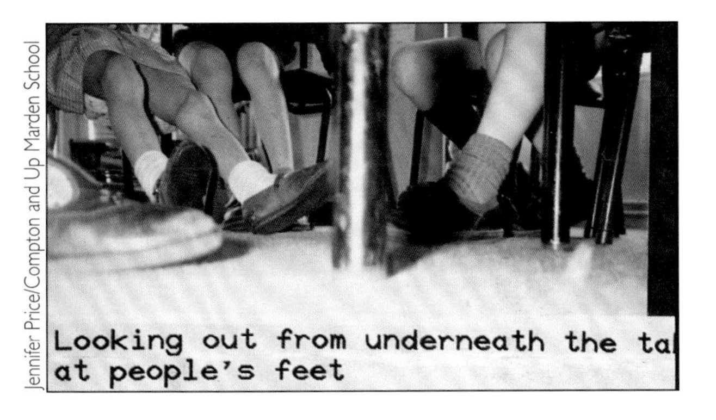

Jennifer Price/Compton and Up Marden School

The bigger picture

The art curriculum now recognises the importance of developing visual literacy, in other words a language through which to talk about how pictures convey meaning.

The way we choose to take a photograph will depend on the context in which we want it to be seen, and is nearly always influenced by the wealth of images that we see around us in our daily lives. We also make decisions which affect the meaning of an image. Some of the choices we make are aesthetic in terms of elements such as: the use of lighting; composition; the choice of colour or black and white film; how colour is used in the image; how forms balance, or not, within the frame; the use of blur, etc. Whether taking a photograph ourselves to be included in the family album, or looking at an existing photograph, such as an advertisement, these images are likely to conform to certain codes and conventions. All art forms have their own visual conventions but, because of its abundance in our culture, photography is likely to be the medium that children are most familiar with in terms of visual arts and therefore find easiest to decipher. ■

'Photo-media studies'

At Bournhall JMI School, Hertfordshire, a project was established that sought to develop an understanding of visual images in terms of how they are made, how they convey meanings and how the viewer understands them.[3] Meaning is conveyed through photographs in very powerful ways and images are often cropped to manipulate or reinforce their meaning. The project also introduced children to ways in which the meaning of an image can be altered depending on the context in which it is seen. Context can include the use of text, as it anchors the meaning of an image, but can also be affected by the way individuals view the image and the knowledge they bring to it depending on their sex, age or cultural background. It is important that children are encouraged to become critically aware of this medium, questioning images they see around them rather than just accepting them. ■

'Photo-media studies' activities

Looking at the whole picture

- Using a number of sheets of black sugar paper cut a window in each sheet in the same place but gradually increase the size of the windows. Working with the whole class use a large photograph from a newspaper or magazine and cover the image with the sheets of black sugar paper, with the sheet with the smallest window on top.
- Ask the children what they can see through the window and what they think might be happening in the photograph as a whole.
- Remove the top sheet of sugar paper to reveal more of the photograph and ask the children the same questions again to see if their ideas have changed.
- Continue in this way until the whole image is exposed. This is a popular way to introduce the concept that a photograph can represent only a select view of a situation and if we could see the wider picture it might alter our understanding of the scene. ■

Imagine a bigger picture

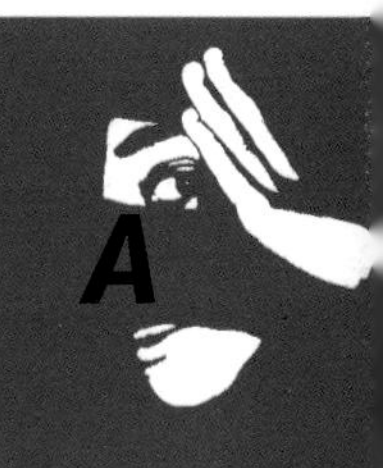

- Hand out parts of found images from newspapers and magazines and ask the children to stick them in the middle of a blank piece of paper. They should then give their picture a title. Then ask them to draw what they imagine might be outside the frame. Once their drawings are complete ask them to title their pictures again. As with the first activity this will highlight how a photograph can be 'cropped' to show the subject in a particular way. ■

Bournhall JMI School

Art

A moment in time

- Using parts of found images or photocopies stuck in the middle of a blank piece of paper ask the children to draw what they imagine was happening just before and just after the photograph was taken. This will illustrate how a photograph is just a moment in time. ■

Bournhall JMI School

Text anchors meaning

- Select a number of news photographs from a newspaper and photocopy them with any accompanying text obscured. Make enough copies so that each child has one and ask them to write a caption to go with it. They could also write from where they think their photograph might have originated, in other words the context in which it might have been found.
- Ask the children to read out the text they have written and compare the different captions created for the same photograph and their thoughts on their original context. ■

Art

Context

- Working as a class and using one photograph as an example begin by telling the children that it came from a magazine and ask them how they think it might have been used, that is, whether it had a story accompanying it or just a caption. Using the same photograph tell the children that you made a mistake and it actually came from a newspaper. See if their interpretation of the image changes. These exercises can provide clear examples of the ways in which the context of a photograph can effect its meaning. ■

Further activities

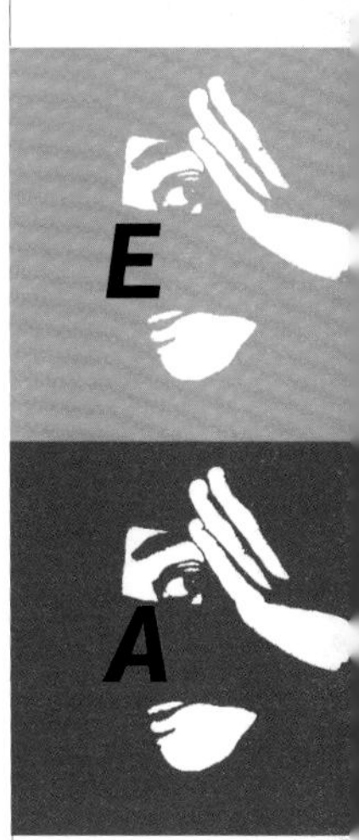

- Explore the ways in which lighting can effect an image. Ask the children to use an anglepoise lamp to try lighting each other from the side, below, above, behind and in front, and by bouncing the light off a white wall or piece of card. They could photograph each different lighting set-up and make a note so they know how each effect was achieved.
- Using a selection of photographs taken by a variety of photographers ask the children to look at them carefully in terms of shape and form, for example it may be that a photograph uses diagonals in such a way as to draw your eye to a certain point in the image. Having studied different examples the children can then try composing their own photographs to apply what they have learnt.
- Ask the children to look for a variety of patterns and shapes that occur within the school, playground or locality. These can then be photographed using colour print film and the resulting enprints enlarged on the photocopier. If a number of copies are made of each image then the work can be extended to create more complex images. The image shown here was created by children at Oliver Goldsmith Junior School, London.[4]
- Find an advertising image that makes strong use of colour and ask the children why they think that particular colour has been chosen. This activity will link well with the next two projects in the chapter. ■

Oliver Goldsmith Junior School

Resources

- Selection of found images from newspapers, magazines and books
- Black sugar paper, plain white paper and glue
- Access to a photocopier

How do I feel?

One of the key aspects of visual literacy is to teach children the language through which images communicate meaning. Once they can 'read' this visual language they will be far better equipped to 'write' with it, in other words they will develop their ability to communicate through their own images. Photography can be a powerful tool for self-expression, as many of the images in this book show, and from the simple activity of creating a self-portrait to the more challenging task of articulating complex feelings through a visual medium children can take control of the image-making process to put themselves in the picture. ■

'Ourselves'

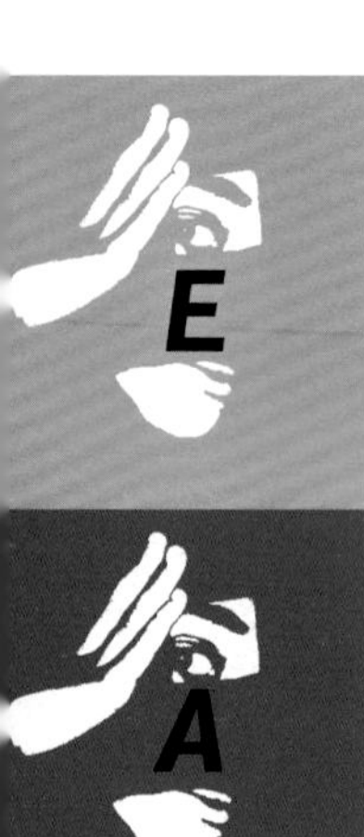

At Desmond Anderson First School, West Sussex, children used portrait photography to communicate a range of moods and feelings they had experienced.[5] In particular they studied the work of photographer, Jo Spence, who uses the medium as a form of therapy, exploring experiences and emotions through self-portraits. Once a child had chosen the mood they wanted to express decisions had to be made regarding facial expression and camera angle. The moods captured in the their photographs were then amplified through the use of shape and colour. Working in this way proved valuable for individual children's development of colour-handling and mark-making skills. ■

'Ourselves' activities

- Begin with a class discussion about feelings and emotions and ask the children about experiences that have provoked particular feelings for them.
- Once every child has identified an emotion they have felt ask them to imagine how they look when they are feeling this way and to practise the appropriate facial expressions.
- Each child should then plan how they can express their chosen feeling in a photograph. This might involve sketching how they want the photograph to look in terms of facial expression. They could consider the camera angle to use to increase the mood of the picture, for example, to make someone look scared or vulnerable you would photograph them looking down from above. They should also consider the general composition of their photograph.
- The children should work in pairs and these plans or sketches can be given to their partners enabling them to photograph their subject in the desired way.

- Often even very young children can make strong associations between feelings and colours. Once the film has been processed ask them to think of how they might extend the mood of their image by incorporating particular colours to create a border or background for their photograph.
- The photographs and drawings can then be montaged together. ■

Michelle Vogel/Desmond Anderson First School

Resources

- 35mm compact camera and colour print film
- Paper, drawing materials and paints

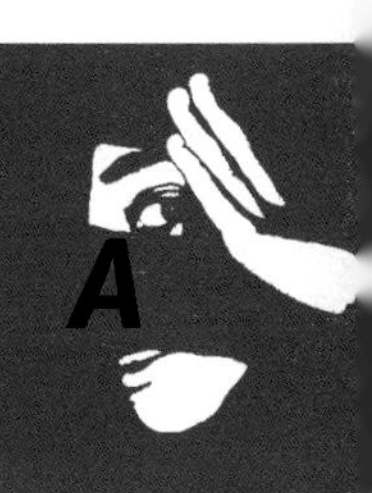

'Eye to eye – the bullying project'

In Nottingham a group of artists working under the name Circle Projects have devised an arts-based initiative that has successfully tackled bullying in local schools. The overall aim of their approach, called 'Eye to eye', is to enable children to articulate their views, experiences and feelings vividly and directly through arts activities, and photography has proved to be an accessible medium through which to achieve these aims.

Children from The Elms Primary School, Nottingham, took part in 'Eye to eye' and used photographs to freeze moments from role-play activities.[6] Using facial expressions and body language they explored role-playing as a means of developing positive strategies to deal with conflict within the classroom, the playground and beyond. They photographed each other during the activity in order to capture the most important aspects of these conflicts and their solutions. Being photographed helped the children understand the power and subtlety of facial expression and gesture, and provided a good structure for focusing their ideas.

In other schools 'Eye to eye' has been developed to explore the use of symbolism with children, avoiding literal or stereotypical

PSHE
RE

E

A

Art

The Elms Primary School

The Elms Primary School

The Elms Primary School

representations of both bully and victim. This has been achieved through the production of visual images and the writing of poetry, and in both cases the children have imagined the bully or victim in the abstract sense as something other than a person. Colour was found to have strong associations for them and by using it as the key component in their photographs they managed to create sophisticated images that powerfully express their feelings around these issues. It is important that time is spent laying the groundwork for a project of this kind, discussing issues of identity, fear and anxiety, prejudice and tolerance as well as different forms of bullying, before embarking on the practical activities. ■

The Elms Primary School

'Eye to eye' activities

- After discussions with the class focusing on bullying ask the children to think about the role of bully or victim in an abstract sense. For example, if a bully were a colour what colour would they be? They can then write short poems imagining the bully or victim in this way (or construct photographs that use colour as a strong visual element as in the PSHE and RE chapter).

'I think that if a colour could be a bully
It would be red with anger and madness ...'

'A victim's colour is blue
The colour stands for fear ...'

'Bullies are like a thunder storm
Loud and unpleasant to listen to
Like a cactus or an electric chair
Waiting to hurt and upset you ...'

'It wears a jumper with a small grey spot on it
– Loneliness.'

- The poems can then be used to develop role-plays, with the children imagining themselves as the bully or victim in this abstract sense. This can be an effective way of de-personalising experiences or feelings, thus reducing the possibility of children feeling vulnerable or embarrassed.
- The resulting images can be used to analyse different scenarios that arose through role-play and to highlight points of conflict and resolution. They can also act as a useful resource for other teachers working around issues of this kind with their classes. ■

John Clifford Primary School

Resources

- 35mm camera and colour print film
- Resources for projection images, see PSHE and RE chapter

Painting with light

In the 1920s photographers and artists began to see the potential of photography as a new creative medium, breaking away from pictorialism and using the process to experiment with graphic shapes and patterns in order to create abstract images. It was at this time that Man Ray pioneered experimental techniques such as photograms, or 'rayographs' as he liked to call them, and through direct chemical means created images that challenged the conventions of both art and photography. ■

'Photo-batik'

At Normanton First School, Wakefield, children experimented with the technique known as photo-batik.[7] This involves 'painting' directly on to photographic paper with thick hand cream to prevent the photographic chemicals used reaching certain areas, in a similar way that wax and paint are used to make traditional batik images. The process allows children the freedom to use the medium as they would a paintbrush or pencil, while at the same time illustrating the way in which daylight or artificial light affects light-sensitive material.

Children can also paint on to photographic paper by dipping a paintbrush into the chemicals themselves to create chemograms. If developer is used the areas where it has covered the paper will turn black, and if fixer is used the painted areas on the paper will remain white. Both activities can take place in daylight in the classroom with any age group. For more information about safety procedures for children to follow when working with photographic chemicals see the science chapter. ■

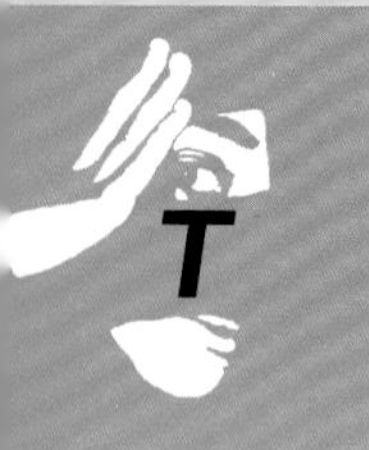

'Photo-batik' activities

- Begin by asking each child to draw a picture or choose a favourite drawing that they have done. They will reproduce this picture in their photo-batik.
- The children should then each be given a sheet of photographic paper. These sheets should be taken out of the box in a black film-changing bag or inside a couple of bin liners to protect the rest of the box from exposure.
- Using their finger, a cotton bud, paintbrush or similar implement the children should apply the hand cream to any areas of their paper that are to stay white, copying their drawing as closely as possible.

Art

Because they are applying white cream to white photographic paper the children might find it helpful if you add food colouring to the hand cream so they can see where they are applying it. They may also find it easier to cover the paper completely in the cream and then scratch out the areas they want to go black.

- Once this has been done they must place the paper in a tray of developer, making sure it is completely covered by the solution and agitate it for the recommended time. Any areas that do not have cream on them will turn black as soon as the paper makes contact with the developer.
- The paper must then be transferred to a tray filled with soapy water in order to wash the cream off and then be rinsed in clean water.
- Fix and wash the print, then dry. ■

Leigh Selway/Normanton First School

Further activities

- The children could apply cream to their hands or feet and then press them on to the photographic paper. The result will be a white hand or footprint on a black background.
- Reverse the picture-making process to create black images on a white background. With this technique cream should be applied to areas that the children want to go black and the paper should be placed in a tray of fixer after the cream has been applied. The cream should then be washed off in soapy water, the paper rinsed and then developed. The results effectively demonstrate the way in which fixer makes photographic paper inactive to light and to developer. ■

Resources

- Multigrade photographic paper (glossy finish)
- Hand cream
- Cotton buds, paint brushes, etc.
- Developer, fixer, water and three trays
- Washing-up liquid mixed with water in a tray (to remove hand cream)
- Tongs
- Plastic gloves

'Strobe pictures'

A strobe picture is a circular symmetrical pattern built up on photographic paper, usually from a single shape. It is a popular activity with children at Woodstock School, Bristol, as spectacular graphic patterns can arise through symmetrical repetition.[8] Depending on the age of the children you are working with you could do the preparation activities for the strobe pictures yourself, or set it as a mathematical task for the children to undertake. Unlike photo-batiks, when creating strobe pictures work must be done in a darkroom using red safelighting or a torch or lamp covered with a red gel. ■

'Strobe pictures' activities

- Cut a circle of black card large enough to cover the photographic paper you are using, and then cut a section from that circle with an angle of 60°. Then cover the cut out section with clear acetate and fix it in place with tape.
- Mark out a rectangle that corresponds to the paper size you are using on a piece of foam board. You should then mark out a circle that corresponds to the black card circle so the children can see where the centre of it should be. You can also mark 60° divisions on the board (the lines will extend underneath the circle) to make it easier when the children are exposing the different sections of the paper.

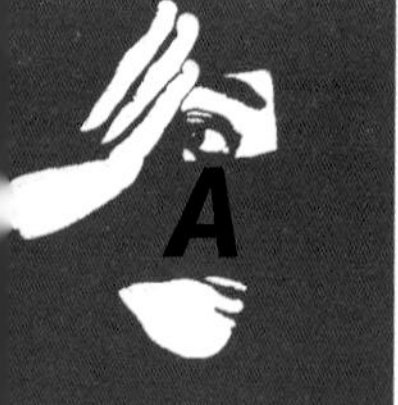

Board with guide marks for placement and 60° rotation

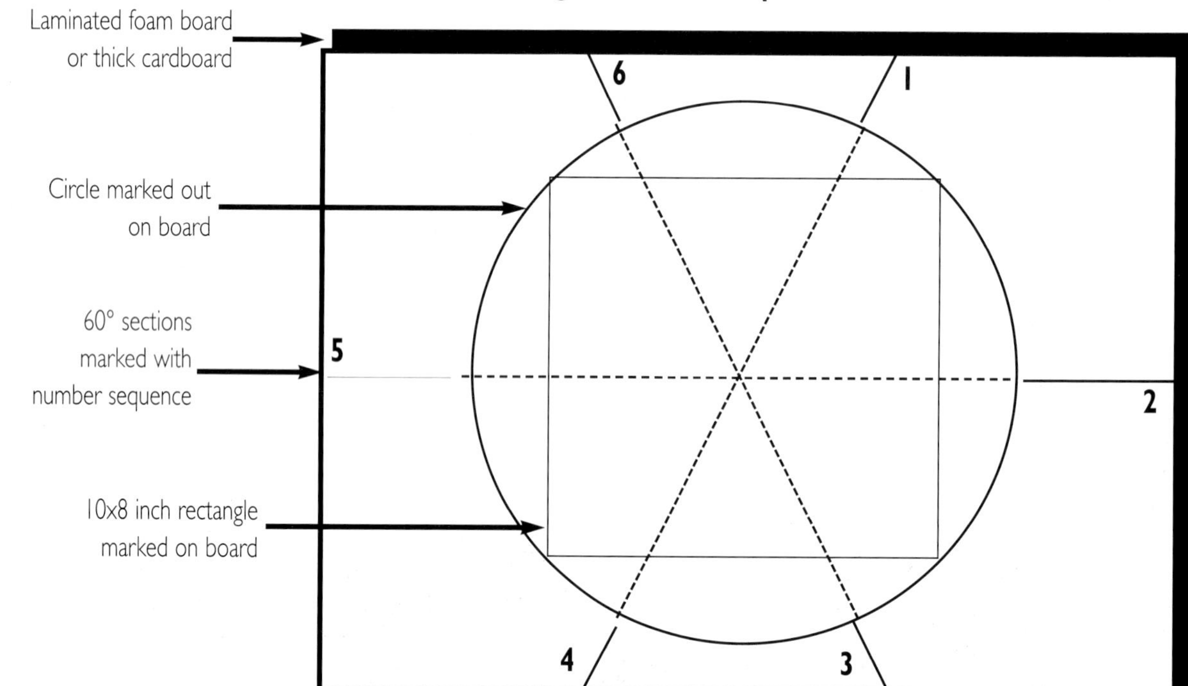

- The children then need to select small objects or shapes to place on the acetate section to produce the repeated pattern.
- In a darkroom position the photographic paper on the foam board using Blu-Tack to keep it in place. Then place the card circle over the paper, inserting a pin through the centre that passes through the photographic paper and fixes the card to the foam board. The card circle will now turn easily, but because the paper is held in place with the Blu-Tack there is no danger of it accidentally moving.
- The children should place their object or shape on the acetate section only, and the paper can then be exposed to light. You will need to experiment to find the correct exposure time.
- The card circle is then rotated 60° to align with the next division marked on the foam board and the paper is exposed again.
- Continue in this way until the whole sheet of paper has been exposed to light – this will be six turns if a 60° angle is being used.
- Remove the card circle and develop the paper in the same way as for an ordinary photogram – developer, rinse, fixer, wash. ■

Joshua/Woodstock School

Resources

- Darkroom
- Multigrade photographic paper
- Black card
- Blu-Tack
- Acetate sheet and tape
- Shape or object to be repeated
- Foam board
- Pin
- Developer, fixer, water and three trays
- Tongs or plastic gloves
- Desk lamp or torch as source of white light
- Red safelight, torch or lamp covered with a red gel

What do I see?

Children have often used cameras as notebooks in art, collecting information to use as source material for drawing and painting activities. Photographs can record fragments of the natural and built environment that cannot be physically brought into the classroom (but they can also record details or the play of light on objects already in the classroom). In this way photography can provide a successful means of developing children's observational skills through taking and using photographs to analyse details and document change. Art is all about looking and because photographs are still images, as opposed to moving images, they are ideally suited for use as study material in the classroom. ■

'Creatures'

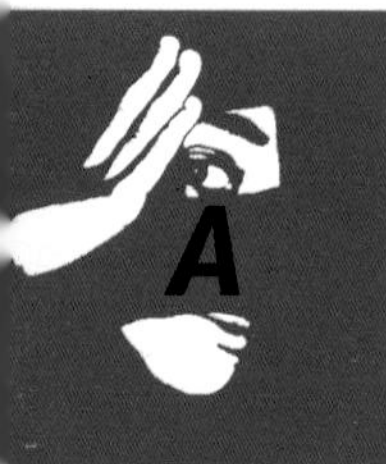

At Rogate School, West Sussex, children used cameras to produce close-up photographs recording detailed parts of creatures such as fish and crabs.[9] The children chose the detail they wanted to photograph and the teacher helped set the camera on a tripod to ensure sharp results. Once developed the photographs were used as a reference for drawing and painting activities and were then kept and used as part of a permanent image bank. ■

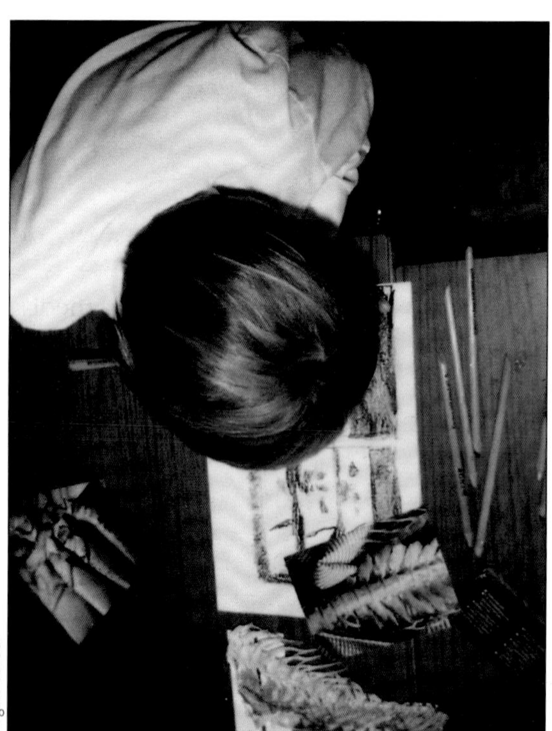
Rogate School

Danielle Bleach/Rogate School

Danielle Bleach/Rogate School

'Creatures' activities

- Ask the children to choose something they have seen in the classroom or the school grounds that they would like to draw. The focus could be on something natural or artificial.
- They should then study whatever they have chosen close up and decide on a position from which they would like to photograph it.
- Using a camera with a close-up filter or lens they should then take their photograph. If working with very young children it might be helpful if the camera is set up on a tripod.
- The resulting images can then be used as source material for drawing and painting. ■

Further activities

- Each photograph could be photocopied a number of times and, by looking at the patterns and shapes that develop when the copies are laid side by side, the children can create new images.
- The contemporary artist, Andy Goldsworthy works with natural elements, for example, sticks, leaves and ice, to make sculptures which are then photographed. The children could refer to his work and create designs, sculptures or pictures with their found objects and record these on film. ■

Resources

- 35mm camera and close-up filter or lens
- Colour print film
- Tripod

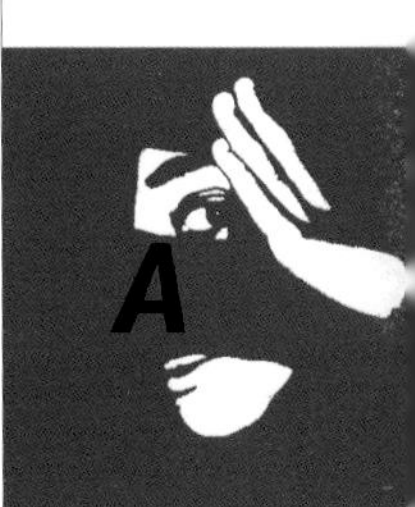

'Movement'

Southgate First School, West Sussex, used the study of movement and time to develop a series of photographic-based art activities that would improve children's skills in observation and visual interpretation, and introduce them to the work of other artists.[10] To begin with they embarked on similar activities to those outlined in the 'Photo-media studies' project, working with found images and drawing what they imagined to be outside the frame. Questions were also raised as to what might have happened just before or after a photograph was taken. The children then studied examples of the work of photographers, such as Eadwærd Muybridge, that dealt with movement and time before developing their own work. In the late 1800s Muybridge invented a technique whereby he could record a movement sequence in a series of still photographs, enabling detailed observation of both humans and animals 'in flight'. Photography of this kind highlights the close relationship the medium has with both art and science. ■

'Movement' activities

- Use the work of Eadwærd Muybridge in order to illustrate how movement can be documented in photographic sequences then divide the class into groups and ask each group to devise a simple movement sequence that they could document in five or six photographs. They could use storyboards to plan the sequence and to help their decision as to the precise moment at which each photograph should be taken.
- In some of his 'joiner' montages David Hockney depicts the passing of time, for example, when a person appears several times in a joiner but in different parts of the room or picture space. Having shown the children some of Hockney's work, divide them into groups and ask them to take a number of photographs that can be combined to create one large image that suggests the passing of time. A good number might be ten to twelve, but this will depend on the resources you have available.
- If you have access to a 35mm camera with manual controls and a tripod the children can experiment with slow shutter speeds to record their classmates' movements. These might be small head or facial movements, movement of the hands or arms, or of the whole body. The photographs will show blur where the movement has taken place. ■

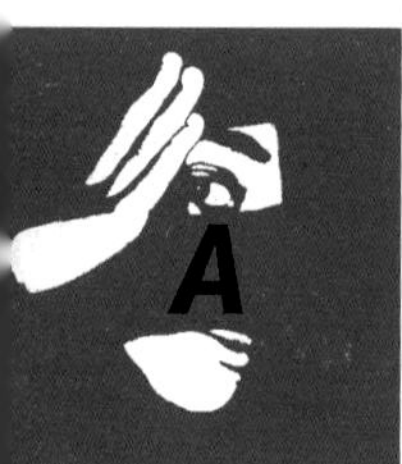

Daniel Sanderson/Southgate First School

Southgate First School

Southgate First School

Resources

- Images of movement and the passing of time by photographers such as Eadwærd Muybridge, David Hockney, etc.
- 35mm manual camera and colour print film
- Tripod

'A picture you can walk into'

Children used photographs to explore their surroundings as part of a collaborative project in Northumberland involving an advisory teacher, an artist and six First Schools.[11] Held over a week in a spare classroom at one of the participating schools, groups of 20 to 24 children took part for one day each. Each group built on and extended the work of earlier groups to create a cumulative piece that took the form of an environmental installation linking drawing, photography and computer imagery.

The school is close to a beach and each group spent the first part of the morning there, drawing and taking photographs that focused on details within the landscape encouraging them to look more closely at their surroundings. As a guide they were asked to look for four things: an interesting shape, interesting lines, a made object and something which showed evidence of presence. They also made drawings in the sand using found materials such as stones, seaweed and water. This introduced the process of working on a large scale while encouraging the children to use the materials present in this environment to represent it.

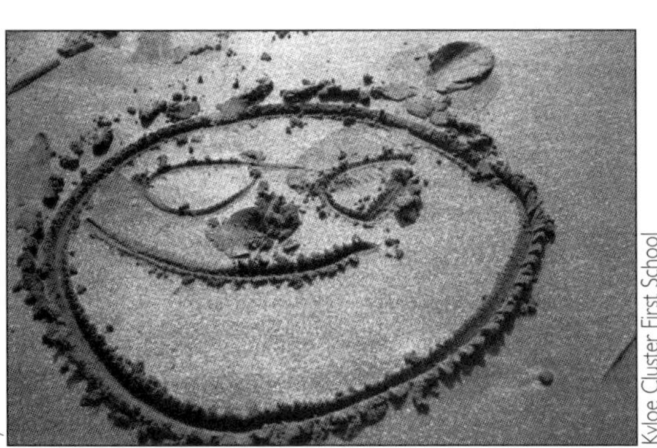
Kyloe Cluster First School

Kyloe Cluster First School

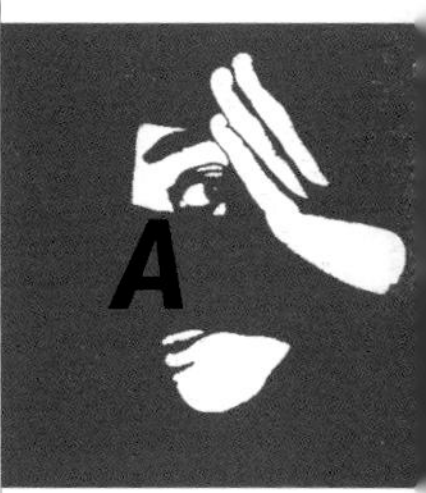

Once back at the school children were asked to design a 'three-dimensional picture' using the drawings, photographs and objects that they had bought back with them as a starting point. Comparisons can be made between this concept of installation and the environments that primary teachers sometimes create within their own classrooms, for example, turning the space into a tropical rainforest as part of a class topic. The children had used black and white film at the beach and, in order to overcome the problem of producing images with no darkroom and not much time, the films were developed in the classroom during the lunch break. Technology was then introduced in a servicing role, using a computer and screen to view the negatives as positives, enabling the children to select quickly and easily the images that they wanted to have printed. These were then digitised and printed on ordinary A4 paper and some were enlarged on the photocopier to the sizes the children required for the installation. For information on digitisers and computers see the technical tips chapter. ■

Art

'A picture you can walk into' activities

- Once you have identified an environment to focus on organise a class visit taking a range of art materials and cameras.
- Allow enough time for the children to explore the environment thoroughly and then ask them to use a variety of approaches to record what they have seen. This may involve talking to each other about what they see, hear, smell or feel and could involve specific tasks for their picture-taking. Looking for something that showed evidence of presence on the beach provoked much thought amongst the children in Northumberland and the images they produced included marks left by the wind and tide, cobwebs, bird-droppings, the remains of a beach fire and parts of an abandoned vehicle.

Kyloe Cluster First School

Kyloe Cluster First School

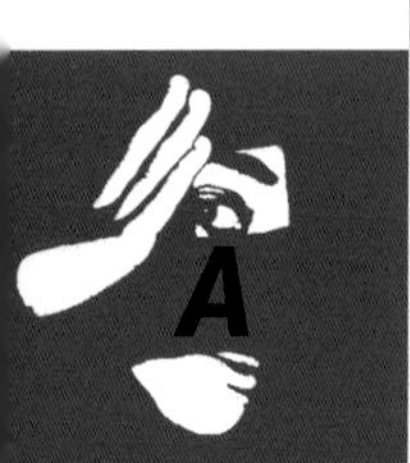

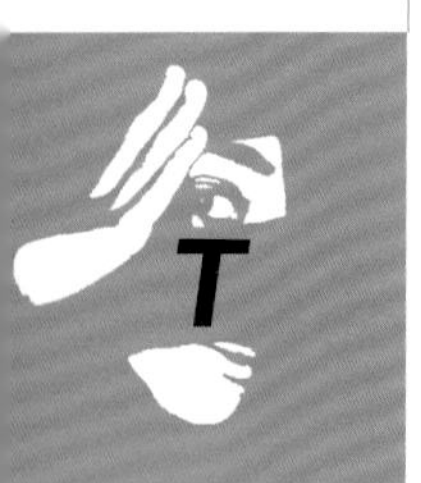

- If you decide to produce a similar large-scale environmental installation a space should be identified and the class should spend time in it thinking about how they might make the transition from their two-dimensional photographs and drawings to a three-dimensional construction.
- Once the photographs are ready for viewing ask the children to select those that best express their response to the environment. If the class are working together on the activity ownership of images becomes irrelevant as everyone's work will be combined. The children may need the opportunity to alter the scale of their photographs and drawings depending on their use within the final piece and photocopies are the cheapest and most accessible way of achieving this.
- Photographs can be taken to document the finished 'three-dimensional picture' before it is dismantled. ■

Kyloe Cluster First School

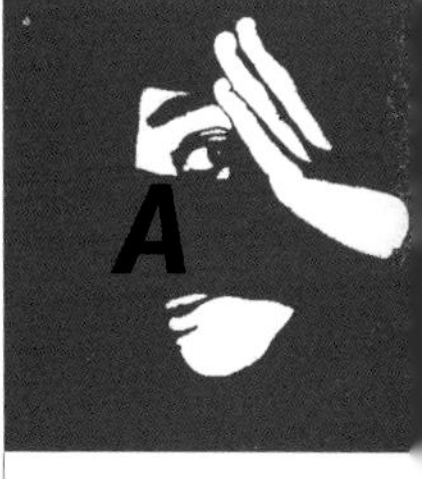

Further activities

- Tape-recorders could be taken on the visit to your chosen environment and sounds particular to that place recorded and then played back in the installation space.
- Slide film could also be used allowing the possibility of projection within the space, or images could be photocopied on to acetate and overhead projectors used to project them.
- The installations of artists such as Keith Piper, Mona Hatoum and a site-specific work such as Rachel Whiteread's 'House' can be referenced by the children to extend their ideas for working in a three-dimensional space. ■

Resources

- 35mm camera (ideally with close-up filter or lens)
- Colour and/or black and white film
- Drawing materials and paper
- A suitable space to create the environmental installation

Art

'Hidden histories'

This cross-curricular project is the result of a short residency arranged by The Photographers' Gallery involving an artist in residence working at St Saviour's and St Olave's School for Girls, London.[12] The project illustrates how an exhibition can be used as a starting point for classroom-based work. Although undertaken with Key Stage 3 children the approach will work very well with children at Key Stage 2. The class visited a site-specific installation by artist Marysia Lewandowska at The Photographers' Gallery. The exhibition presented some interesting questions about the nature of photography, its relationship with light and with the gallery space. As well as responding to the installation the girls were encouraged to question the nature of images. Throughout the project a critical and analytical relationship with images was sustained and developed.

The class then developed their own photographic installation with the focus on the hidden history of the school. This history was uncovered through staff members' memories, material evidence such as old photographs, objects and clothing, the school in the present, and through the position of the girls themselves as performers and commentators. When compiled the various sources of this history gave rise to the question: is there one true history or is there a variety of interpretations?

The girls' finished work was placed within the building itself, making use of windows as huge light boxes. In both its content and its presentation this project served to highlight how history can be revealed in the very fabric of a building and how children can be the creators and producers of sophisticated art works. ■

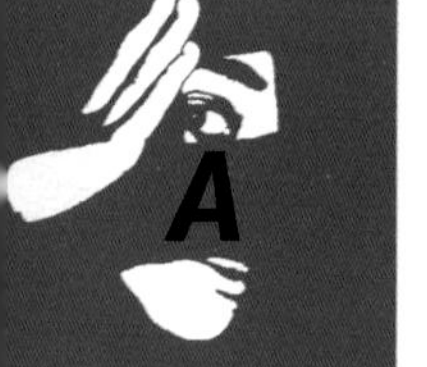

'Hidden histories' activities

- As with the previous project, when creating an installation with children it might be helpful if they could see an example of this kind of work in a gallery setting before they start their own work. If a visit can be arranged devise a questionnaire that the children can fill out during their visit, drawing their attention to the use of the gallery space, how the work makes them feel, what the space is like to be in, whether there are any unusual sounds or smells, etc.
- Once you have decided on the kind of environment you want to create you will need to consider the medium to use, for example, slides, large-scale photocopies or image transfer on to material, and the location where the installation will be constructed. The children can then begin their research for the piece.
- Working in small groups or pairs and taking the example of the history of the school as a focus the children should gather as much visual, written and verbal information as they can about this history. This could be through material evidence such as old photographs, architectural plans, etc. and through interviews recorded with staff members and possibly parents who went to the same school.

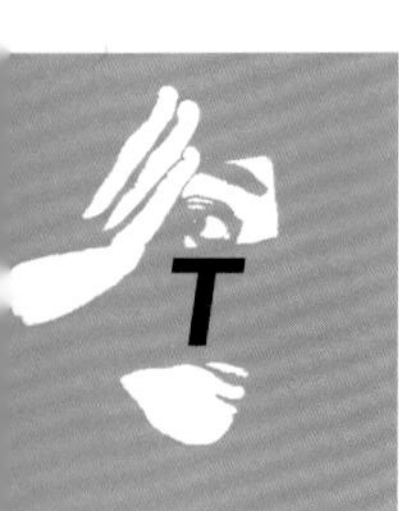

- Depending on the final form of the installation the results of their research can then be copied on to slide, photographed on to print film, photocopied, fed into the computer, etc. and the resulting material brought together to create the finished piece. ■

St Saviour's and St Olave's School for Girls

Resources

- Relevant visual material, and possibly written and verbal information depending on the focus of the project
- 35mm camera, close-up filter or lens
- Colour print or slide films
- Paper, pencils, scissors, etc.
- Tape-recorder and audio tapes for interviews, if applicable
- Photocopier, if applicable
- Slide projector, if applicable

Project credits

1. 'Framing': Barton Hill Junior School, Bristol. Key Stages 1 and 2.
   Kamina Walton, photographer in residence
2. 'Animals': Compton and Up Marden School, West Sussex. Key Stages 1 and 2.
   Jenny Fox, advisory teacher, Anna Fox, photographer, Pauline Buzzing and Esme Mather, class teachers
3. 'Photo-media studies': Bournhall JMI School, Hertfordshire. Key Stages 1and 2.
   Kim Walden, animateur and Margaret Harris, class teacher
4. 'Patterns and shapes': Oliver Goldsmith Junior School, London. Key Stage 2.
   Kamina Walton, photographer in residence
5. 'Ourselves': Desmond Anderson First School, West Sussex. Key Stage 1.
   Jenny Fox, advisory teacher and Louise Haarer, class teacher
6. 'Eye to eye – the bullying project': The Elms Primary School, Nottingham. Key Stage 2.
   Circle Projects: Jo Solomon, Daniel Saul, Karen Rew and Kay Brown
7. 'Photo-batik': Normanton First School, Wakefield. Key Stages 1 and 2.
   Sarah Mumford, advisory teacher
8. 'Strobe pictures': Woodstock School, Bristol. Key Stages 1 and 2.
   Lily Lam, support teacher
9. 'Creatures': Rogate School, West Sussex. Key Stage 1.
   Jenny Fox, advisory teacher and Amanda De Courcy, class teacher
10. 'Movement': Southgate First School, West Sussex. Key Stage 2.
    Jenny Fox, advisory teacher and Yvonne Davis, class teacher
11. 'A picture you can walk into': Kyloe Cluster First School, Northumberland. Key Stage 2.
    Chris Madge, advisory teacher and Helen Smith, arts worker.
12. 'Hidden histories': St Saviour's and St Olave's School for Girls, London. Key Stage 3.
    The Photographers' Gallery, London. Shona Illingworth, artist, Elizabeth Price and Isobel Quinlivan, class teachers and Tracey Barbe, media resources officer ■

Art planning grid

Key Stage	Project	Programme	At1	AT2
1	Framing	1 2c 3 4 d	8ad	7f
1	Animals	1 2a 3 4d	7c 8ade	9b
1	Photo-media studies	1 3	8a 7c 8ef	
1	Ourselves	1 2ac 3	8adef	7be
2	Eye to eye – the bullying project	1 2ac 3	8ade	7f
1	Photo-batik	1 2c 4d 6	7c	
1	Strobe pictures	1 2c 4a	8de	
1	Creatures	1 2bc 3 4acd	7abc 8abcdef	7e
2	Movement	1 2bc 3 4d 5	7c 8abde	7e 9b
2	A picture you can walk into	1 2bc 3 4d	7abcd 8abcdef	7be
2	Hidden histories	1 2c 3 5ab	7bc 8abcde	7ef 9ab

Who am I?

PSHE and RE

Who are we?

Who am I?

This chapter takes the question 'Who am I?' as its central theme because it is in PSHE and RE, more than in any other place in the curriculum, that the focus is on the child rather than a discrete body of knowledge or a set of prescribed skills. The content of both PSHE and RE is shaped by the specific needs of the children in individual schools, but they also share common concerns. Both address the personal, social, moral and spiritual development of the child and should include all aspects of equal opportunities. By taking this approach children are placed at the centre of their learning experience.

The projects and activities within the chapter begin at Key Stage 1 with simple exercises that encourage children to use a camera to represent themselves, and then progress through to more complex approaches at Key Stage 2. The chapter follows a path moving from a child's appearance to their personality, and on to their relation to others. This progression can also act as a useful bridge between the primary level and activities with children at Key Stage 3.

Through photographic practice children can develop study skills by taking on the role of the photographer as well as the subject. Children are required to make decisions and take control of their representations, thus actively exploring the idea of self-identity. At the same time critical thought is developed through the increased understanding of ways in which images can produce meaning, and communication skills are extended through the production of their own images. Interpersonal skills are also enhanced through group-work activities and through children gaining an increased understanding of differences and similarities between themselves and their classmates.

The range of photographic approaches described can be applied at any stage of the child's learning, for example the use of computers to manipulate images digitally need not be restricted to older children but may be introduced at any point in the primary phase. With the focus on the self children can use photography very effectively to look quite literally at themselves and others. Put simply, both PSHE and RE start by asking the question: Who am I? ■

Aims

- To promote the personal and social development of the child, starting with the child.
- To help children to understand themselves and others, which in turn will enable them to contribute to society as informed, responsible and caring individuals.
- To develop an understanding of and to reflect on beliefs, values and traditions, individuals, communities, societies and cultures.
- To enhance spiritual, moral, cultural and social development.

Myself

A logical starting point for the activities in this chapter is to focus on the child's sense of self. It is likely that their only experience of self-image will have been constructed for them through photographs taken by members of their family or by the school photographer. Enabling children to create images of themselves and each other will engage their interest and place them firmly at the centre of their own learning experience. ■

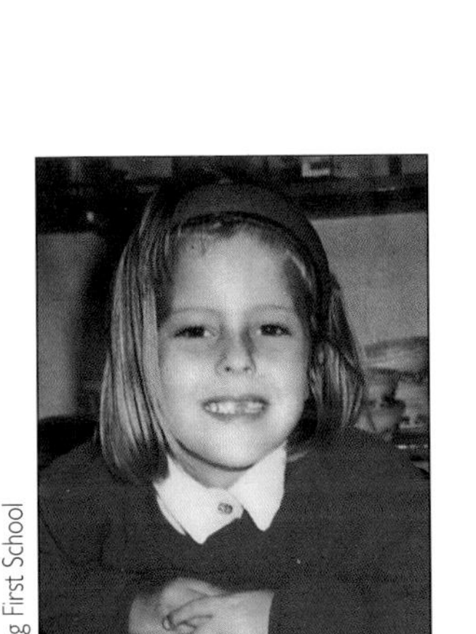
Jade/Lee Brigg First School

'Ourselves'

At Lee Brigg First School, West Yorkshire, children were introduced to the concept of picturing themselves when they were given the task of creating a book about their class.[1] As a starting point, the children practised closing one eye to look through the camera's viewfinder. They then worked with a partner using a cardboard frame to look through in order to plan how they would take their photograph. A Polaroid camera was used for instant results but this project can be done as effectively with a compact camera and ordinary colour print film. ■

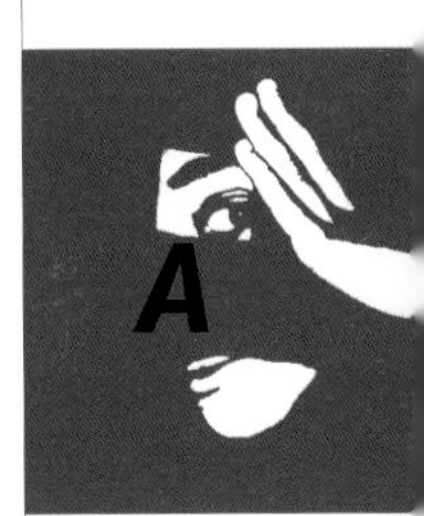

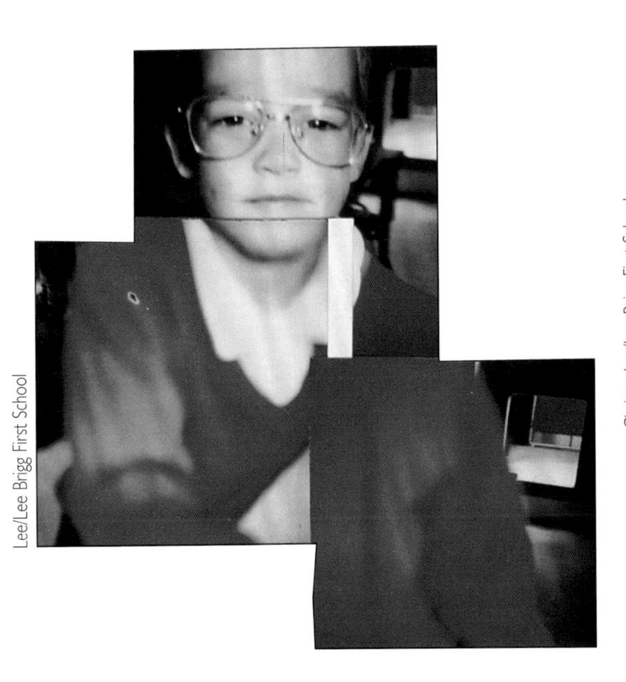
Lee/Lee Brigg First School

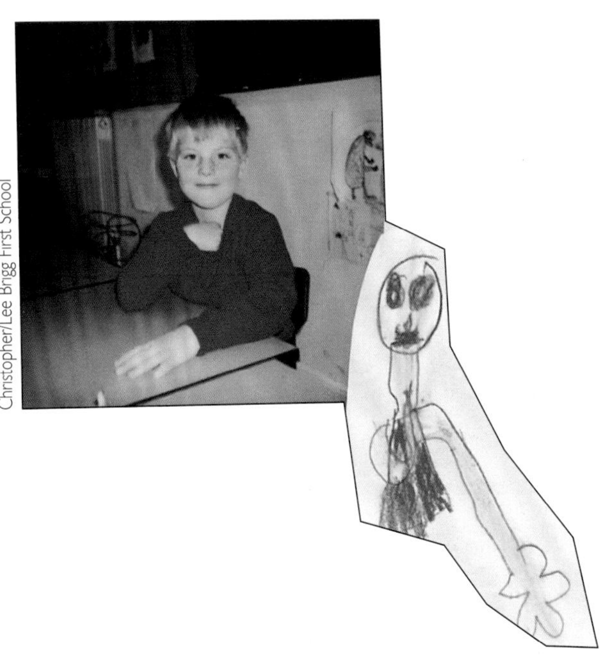
Christopher/Lee Brigg First School

'Ourselves' activities

- Using a card or plastic viewfinder to look through, ask the children to work in pairs to plan a photograph of their partner. They should consider how they will frame their photo, whether to take a close-up portrait of their partner's face or head and shoulders, or whether to include part or all of their body. They should also consider what they can see in the background.
- Using colour print or Polaroid film they can create their portrait by taking one image or by taking two or three that overlap to make a composite picture.
- Once they have done this ask them to write a brief statement about themselves to accompany their photograph, and to draw a self-portrait.
- There is scope for developing this work further by asking children to think about the photograph in relation to the drawing – what have they chosen to include or exclude, have they concentrated on particular features, etc? ■

Resources

- 35mm compact camera or Polaroid camera
- Colour print film or Polaroid film
- Paper and pencils

What do I look like?

Photography can provide a means of exploring our identity in relation to our appearance, for example: what we wear, our facial expressions, body language and our emotions. It is useful to look at the ways in which our image is constructed for us and to discuss with the class whether they are happy with these visual representations of themselves. What do the photographs tell us about the child and what information is excluded? When are photographs taken and when are they not taken? ■

'Hospital project': Part I

Myself and My Environment was the title of a collaborative photographic project between The Photographers' Gallery and Chelsea and Westminster Children's Hospital School, London.[2] Ten half-day sessions were held in the hospital school with a photographer in residence, working alternately with children in two age groups, 4–9 year olds and 9–16 year olds. It was rare to see the same children on more than one occasion so each session had to be self-contained. Over the course of the workshops children were introduced to a range of photographic techniques such as photograms, photo-batik and cyanotypes through which they were encouraged to explore details or parts of their bodies. ■

'Hospital project' activities

- **Batik prints**
  By generously rubbing hand cream on to the soles of their feet or their palms or fingers, children can create images on photographic paper that are, in effect, their own personal signatures. The same method can be used to draw images directly on to the photographic paper using a cotton bud, paintbrush or finger. ■

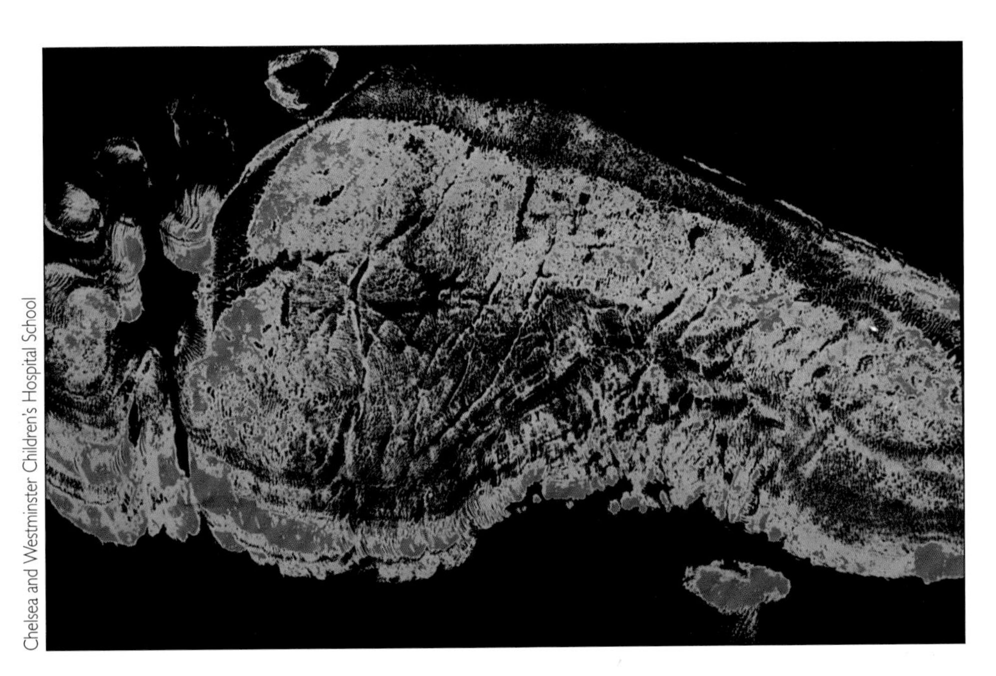

Chelsea and Westminster Children's Hospital School

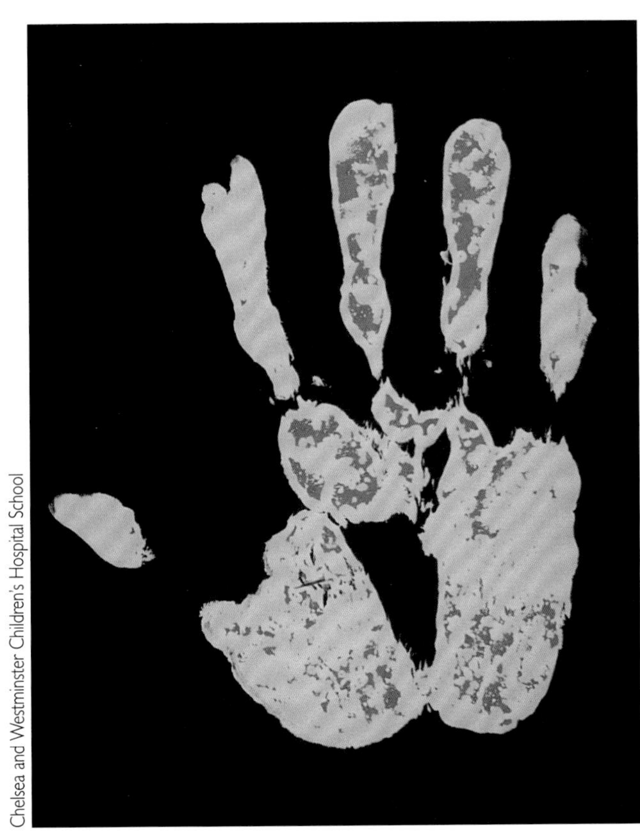

Chelsea and Westminster Children's Hospital School

Resources

- For detailed information see art chapter

'I dream of being': Part I

As part of a term's photography project, children at Camp JMI School, St Albans, used a photocopier to construct a composite identity, some choosing to jigsaw pieces together from head to foot and others just focusing on parts of themselves.[3] Through this process they gradually began to understand how self-image is constructed – that it is not only how we appear physically, but also that the clothes we wear and the possessions we own are all chosen to express something about ourselves. The following activities illustrate one of a variety of approaches to exploring representations of the self other than through traditional portraiture. ■

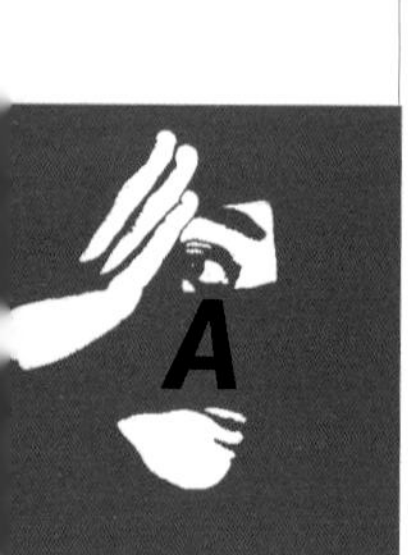

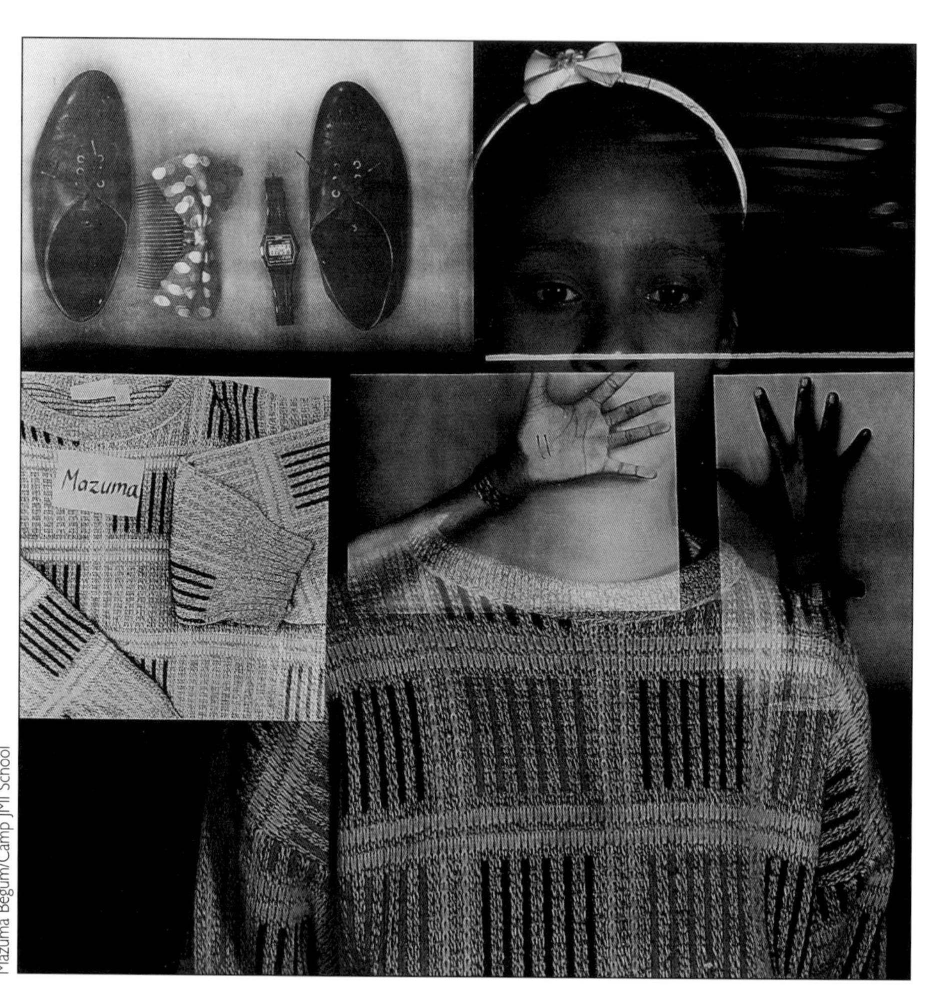

Mazuma Begum/Camp JMI School

'I dream of being' activities

- Ask the children to identify different parts of themselves such as hair, articles of clothing, footwear and accessories that make up their self-image.
- Once they have selected the different elements each one can be photocopied and single or multiple copies can be made.
- These photocopies can then be jigsawed together to make composite self-portraits. ■

Resources

- Children's personal possessions
- Photocopier
- Existing portrait photographs

Who am I and who could I be?

Once children have developed a sense of self in relation to appearance a further development would be to allow them to explore their personality. Photography can be used to call on children's imaginations and sense of fantasy to map out their dreams, hopes and aspirations. This opens the door to endless possibilities for image-making using a wider variety of techniques and provides children with an opportunity to explore aspects of themselves of which they may be unaware.

When developing this kind of work around self-portraits it is useful if children create their own scrap-book of images, whether found or self-generated. However, it is important to be aware that there are limited found images that children will have access to and this may affect the resulting work. ■

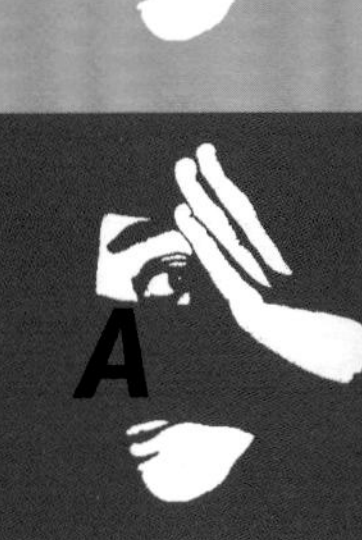

'Clothes and stories'

Children at Londonmeed CP School, West Sussex, moved away from the self at the start of their project and used images of clothing as a focal point for their photography and painting activities.[4] They brought in photographs from their family albums and the class discussed what people were wearing in them and what they were doing. They had to think about whether the clothes had anything to do with the activity or event being represented.

The teacher asked a series of questions that encouraged exploration of the associated meanings and functions which clothes have in our society, and to help the children develop awareness of the ways in which we use clothing for protection, camouflage, group identification, celebration, display, etc. The focus was then bought back to the self and each child brought in their favourite clothes to be photographed in. ■

'Clothes and stories' activities

- Looking at a range of images of people ask the children a series of questions in order to develop awareness of the ways in which clothing is used, for example: Who would wear these clothes? When? Where? What would they do in them? What are they made of?
- They could then bring in their favourite clothes, whether casual wear, fancy dress, sportswear, etc. with the intention of being photographed by their partner in their chosen outfit. They could also consider how they want to look regarding facial expression and

body language – whether friendly, angry, sad, happy, excited, etc.

- Once decisions have been made as to how they want their portrait to look ask the children to photograph their partner, either using the camera handheld or set up on a tripod, again taking into consideration camera distance, angle, composition, etc.
- When you have had the films developed ask the children what they think of their images, and, if possible, to give reasons as to why they like or dislike them.

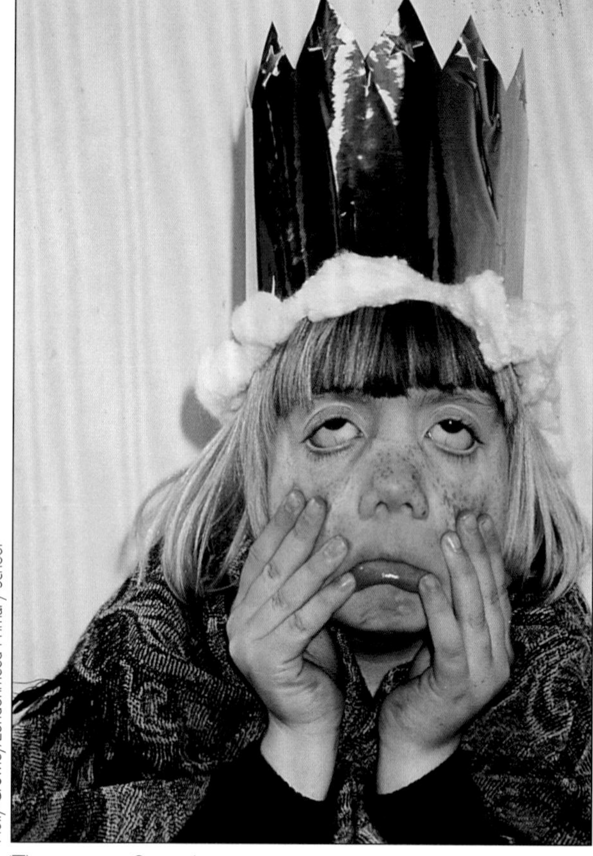

Holly Crowley/Londonmeed Primary School

'The grumpy Queen'

Holly Crowley/Londonmeed Primary School

- The photographs can then be photocopied and the children encouraged to use a variety of drawing materials to create backgrounds for their portraits. Books on Impressionist painters, children' s book illustrations and other source material could be used to help them develop their ideas.
- The children could then write or tell a story about the characters they have created in their images. ■

Further activities

- Ask the children to photograph the different types of clothes worn by people working in and around the school.
- Collect a broad range of press and media photographs of a famous figure, such as the Queen, that show the person wearing a variety of clothing. Ask the children to guess where the person is and what they are doing according to the type of clothes they are wearing. With older children you could extend the activity further to discuss types of photograph and their purpose, for example, formal portrait, paparazzi shots. ■

Resources

- Found images of people wearing a range of clothing
- Dressing-up clothes
- 35mm camera
- Colour print film
- Tripod and cable release – optional
- Drawing materials and paper

'I dream of being': Part 2

The children at Camp JMI School, St Albans, continued their exploration of self-image by using photography playfully to map out their thoughts, dreams, nightmares and fantasies.[5] The project involved collecting photographic images of places they would like to visit and people they would like to meet or even become. Slide film was used to copy these images and the results were then projected on to a plain wall so that the children could interact with them. By wearing white clothing their bodies acted as a small screen and they could almost become part of the image. They were then re-photographed within their new environment or with their altered persona.

In a similar way acetates were used to draw on to, allowing the children to create any image they wanted and these were then projected on to the wall. Working in this way requires careful planning before the children begin drawing as they have to envisage how they can put themselves into their design. It is also possible to photocopy directly on to acetate and this can be used as an alternative way of projecting found imagery, although it should be remembered that if using the school photocopier the images will be in black and white. ■

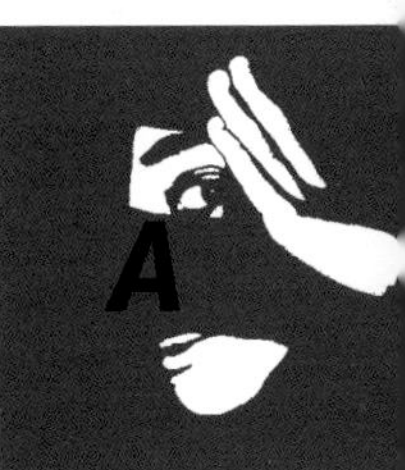

Sarah Hotee/Camp JMI School

'I dream of being' activities

- Using any available magazines, newspapers, books or catalogues ask the class to select images of places they would like to go or people they would like to meet or be. This may involve straightforward cutting out or may call for access to a photocopier if children want to use images from books.
- The next stage of the project is to photograph each selected image on to slide film. If it is possible to borrow a copy stand this will make the process much easier – a local teachers' centre may have one – otherwise find a wall or table in the classroom where there is plenty of available light and, ideally using a tripod, re-photograph the images filling as much of the frame as possible. Depending on the set-up used, the children may be able to do this themselves, or you may have to do it for them.

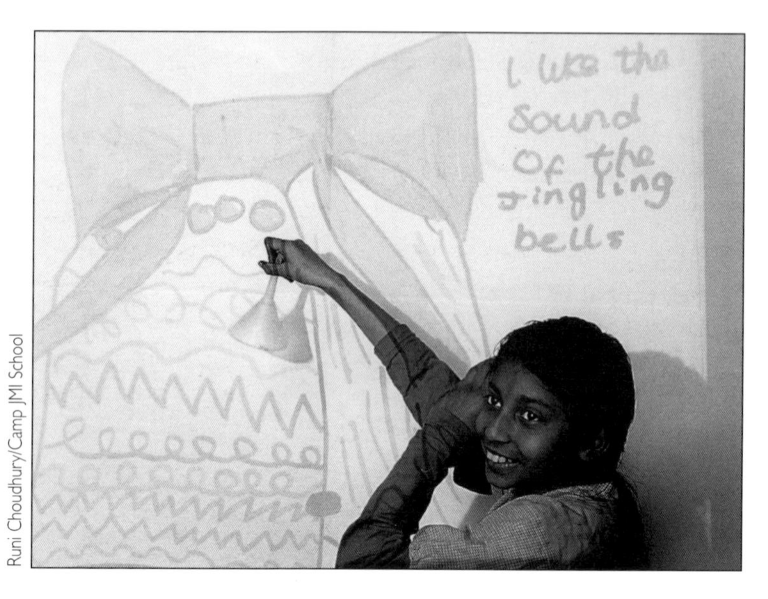

Runi Choudhury/Camp JMI School

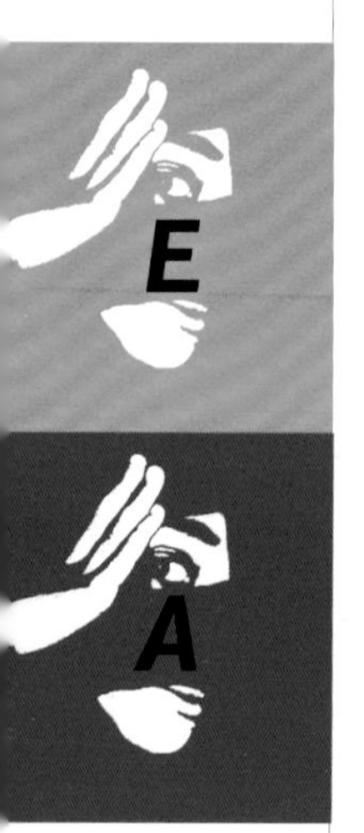

- Ask the class to bring in white clothing and, once the film has been processed, project each image in a darkened room and get each child to place themselves within their image. They should consider where they can be most clearly seen, but also where they can best relate to the image itself. Once in position you can re-photograph them using slide or print film.
- Alternatively, ask the children to plan drawings that they could project and place themselves within. These will be drawn on acetate but at the planning stage work should be done on paper as this reduces the chance of acetate sheets being wasted. If they are careful they can incorporate a space for themselves within their drawing where they can be clearly seen when the finished acetate is projected.
- Project the finished acetate using an overhead projector (OHP) and, as before, once the child has 'entered' the image they can be re-photographed.
- If they prefer, the children could photocopy found images directly on to the acetate, provided you are using the type that can be safely fed through the photocopier ■

Resources

- Found images
- 35mm compact camera
- Slide film and/or acetates
- White clothing
- Overhead projector
- Photocopier
- Colour print or slide film to document the final images – fast film is required for working with low light

'Digital images'

By giving children access to digital image-making the possibilities for exploring dreams and aspirations are limitless. At Mount Pleasant Junior School, Southampton, children had the opportunity to take portraits using a Canon Ion digital camera as part of their topic 'Light'.[6] The Ion is a still video camera that records images directly on to disk. It can be plugged into a computer and the images taken are imported directly to appear on the screen. The children then manipulated their portraits with the computer software package, *Photoshop*, creating disguises and strange new identities for themselves.

The same software was used at Thomas Jones Primary School, London, for the project 'Digital identities' but here children produced traditional photographic images which were then scanned into the computer.[7] The aim of introducing computer-based image manipulation was to provide hands-on creative access to digital media while enabling the children to become actively involved in using photography and new technology to explore their lives, their experiences and the environments in which they are growing up. As a starting point the class visited The Photographers' Gallery to look at a range of portraits and were asked to look carefully at the backgrounds within the photographs as well as the portraits themselves. By drawing their attention to these backgrounds the children were made aware of the different elements within a portrait that provide information about the subject.

In these two projects an artist or photographer was commissioned to work within the school and they provided the computer equipment for the children to work with. If your school does not have access to a computer with software such as *Photoshop* it may be possible to borrow one from your local teachers' centre or to link up with a local media centre. If neither of these options is feasible then the ideas presented here can be explored using photocopying and traditional cut-and-paste techniques. For more information on computer equipment see technical tips chapter. ■

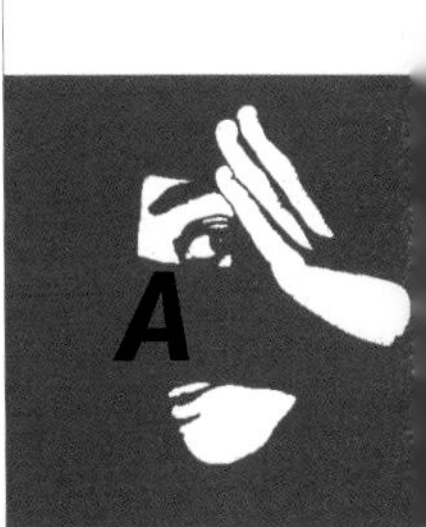

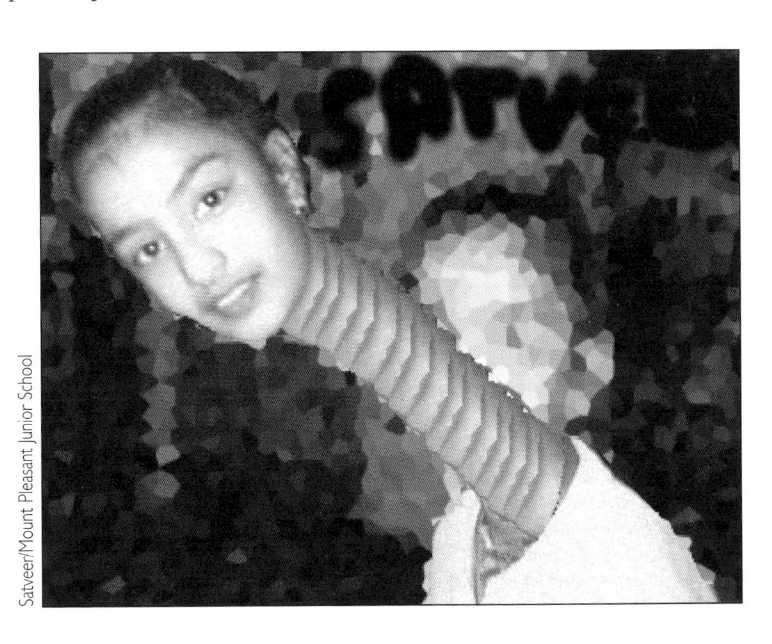

Satveer/Mount Pleasant Junior School

PSHE
RE

PSHE and RE

'Digital images' activities

- There are a number of ways to approach this project depending on the equipment available, the class size and the overall aims. One approach is to organise the class into pairs and ask the children to take a photograph of their partner using a 35mm camera loaded with colour print film. These can be taken in the classroom, playground, or in a studio set-up using a space with a plain background. If available, a Canon Ion camera can be used to save the time and expense of film processing and the need at a later stage for an image scanner.
- To keep the project simple these photographs can then be scanned or the Ion camera can be plugged into the computer and the children can then work independently or in their pairs using the tools available within the software package to explore basic image manipulation. It is a good idea to limit the number of tools they can use so they are not overwhelmed by the options available.

Melissa/Thomas Jones Primary School

A

- Alternatively, after the children have taken their portraits the next stage is to ask them to choose backgrounds in or around the school to photograph for use in their final piece. These could involve favourite places, areas of interest or details such as a piece of graffiti, a flowerbed, etc.
- Then ask each child to select their favourite objects or possessions to photograph. This may involve bringing items in from home such as toys, books or clothing. These items will provide the third element for their final piece and can be photographed in front of a plain background or placed on plain paper.

- When the children have produced photographs for their final piece ask them to experiment by cutting and pasting photocopies of their images (or using extra copies if available) to produce a rough collage. They could also incorporate found images and could duplicate images if necessary. They should think carefully about each element they include, why they have chosen it, and whether it has significance in terms of their identity as a whole.
- Each child should then select the images they need to scan – a portrait, a background and objects or possessions, or, if using an Ion camera they can select from the images that have been imported into the computer.
- They are then ready to begin their own manipulations. By encouraging them to work in pairs, one child can work while the other watches so gaining a more in-depth knowledge of the program's capabilities. When the second child has their turn they may discover possibilities that the first child missed, therefore it is important to allow time for them to go back and make changes to their work. ■

William Goh/Thomas Jones Primary School

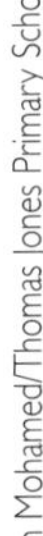

Salah Mohamed/Thomas Jones Primary School

Resources

- Computer with image manipulation software such as *Photoshop*
- 35mm compact camera and colour print film and image scanner or Canon Ion camera
- Found images from home, newspapers, magazines, etc

'Hospital project': Part 2

As part of the collaborative project, *Myself and My Environment*, children at the Royal Brompton Heart and Lung Hospital school site, London, worked with a photgrapher in residence, using photography to create false identity cards.[8] As at the Chelsea and Westminster Children's Hospital, work had to be successfully completed within a half-day session and the aims were to engage children of different ages in the practical production of images. However, at the Royal Brompton an element of fantasy was introduced when children had the opportunity to take on false identities.

The project began with discussion about what ID cards are and what they are used for. The children involved were very familiar with them and could name numerous professions for which they might be issued and as many reasons for their use. Using Polaroid film for instant results, they then took portraits of each other and proceeded to invent an identity that they wished to inhabit. Official-looking name and job title forms were then created on the computer in the style and size of ID cards and the portrait was attached beside the information. These were laminated and a hole was punched out so that a clip attachment could be fixed on and the IDs worn. ■

'Hospital project' activities

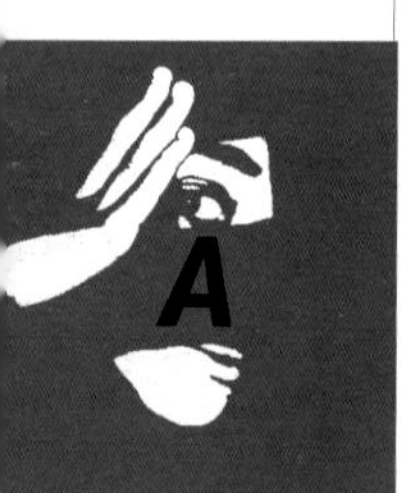

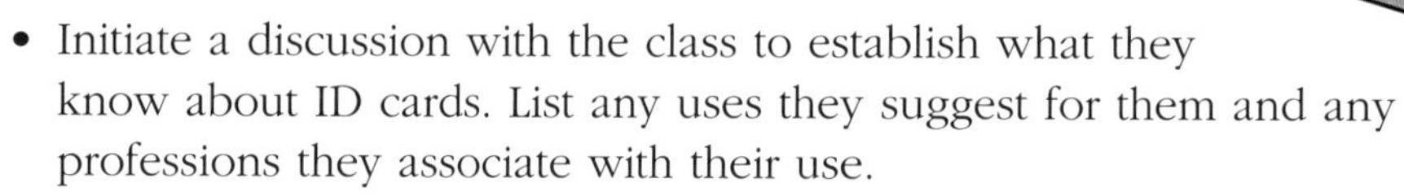

- Initiate a discussion with the class to establish what they know about ID cards. List any uses they suggest for them and any professions they associate with their use.
- Once the children feel the list is complete ask them to choose a false identity that they would like to take on themselves. They could write their idea down and add any information that they feel is relevant to their chosen character or profession.
- Working in pairs the children can then photograph each other in the style of passport photographs, using colour print film.
- While they are waiting for the film to be processed the children can design their ID cards on the computer, leaving a space for their photo but including 'official' information about their new identity.
- Once they have the photos back they can cut themselves out, from the shoulders up, and paste their image to the ID card that they have made.
- These can then be laminated using the school laminator and a safety pin could be stuck to the back, or a hole punched to add a clip attachment, so that the ID cards can be worn. ■

The Royal Brompton Heart and Lung Hospital School site

Resources

- 35mm compact camera
- Colour print film
- Computer for card design
- Laminator
- Safety pins and tape or hole punch and clips

PSHE and RE

Myself and others

By using photography to document areas of importance to them such as lifestyles, cultures and faith, children can begin to explore and understand how they are shaped by the society in which they live and see themselves in relation to other people. The medium thus enables teachers to explore seemingly complex ideas with children.

Given the opportunity to take a camera home to document their lives children can create images that raise issues reflecting the diversity of cultures and family structures represented within the school. By presenting the images to their class these children can be encouraged to talk about their families and where they come from, about their culture and religion, the clothes they wear and the food they eat. In this way photography can be used to demystify difference and highlight any similarities between children and their families, while at the same time create material that the children can identify with and relate to. ■

'Home life'

At Snowsfields Primary School, London, class teachers were having great difficulty finding good multicultural resource material and saw the opportunity for the children themselves to produce teaching resources based on their local environment and daily lives through the introduction of photography.[9] Working with a photographer in residence, children were given cameras to take home for the weekend and were asked to photograph things that they felt best expressed their 'home life'. From twenty exposures each child then selected four to six images to print and these were mounted with captions. The activity involved trusting children with cameras, and this was an important aspect of the project as they responded by treating the equipment and the task with respect. The 'Home lives' project provided an insight into the children's home environment and family life, and also into the place of religion within the family as many of their images focused on religious and cultural icons. The project was also an effective way of strengthening links between school and home by involving parents in their children's classroom work.

At Mount Pleasant Junior School, Southampton, as another element of their topic 'Light', children used photography to explore the significance of light in religion.[10] A group of children were given the opportunity to take a camera home to document Diwali, the Hindu festival of light, and the ways in which light features in the celebrations. From the resulting images and further discussion and research the importance of light in religious ceremonies and celebrations became apparent.

With a project of this nature it is important to begin by writing to parents informing them of the intention of the project and asking their permission for photographs to be taken in their home for future display in the school. ■

PSHE and RE

'Home life' activities

- Begin by organising the children into camera-sharing groups. With careful planning a camera with one roll of film can be shared amongst a number of children – if each child takes the camera home for a few nights or a weekend and uses six photographs then six children could share a 36-exposure film.
- Explain the intention of the project and encourage the children to plan each photograph they might take carefully to prevent wastage of film. It would be useful to provide guidelines as to the type of photographs they might take depending on the emphasis you choose to give the project. These could include family members, friends, meal-times, the home environment and particular places that are special to them, anywhere they might visit in the evenings or at weekends, places of worship or particular celebrations.

Mount Pleasant Junior School

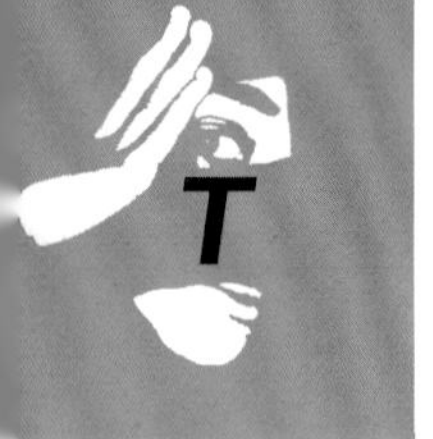

- Once the photographs have been processed ask the children to write short captions for each image that gives it a context. It may be helpful to ask them to imagine they are producing the work for a particular audience who knows nothing about them or their lives. At this stage parents could be involved to help translate captions into children's first language if applicable. ■

It is important to use a camera with a built-in flash so that photographs can be taken indoors and at night. If there is access to a darkroom and black and white film is used children can learn to print their own photographs, thus extending their understanding of light-sensitive materials.

Ashish Regmi/Snowsfields Primary School

'This is me standing on a little chair and this is my God on top of me'

Snowsfields Primary School

Resources

- 35mm compact cameras with built-in flash
- Colour or black and white print film

PSHE
RE

'Eye to eye – the bullying project'

The use of photography can enable teachers to address broader social/health questions, such as bullying, with children. By working with a whole class the focus is taken away from the individual, and project work can develop skills for resolving conflicts which might arise beyond the classroom. In this way teachers can also provide a controlled space in which children can gain a greater insight into and understanding of one another.

In Nottingham practitioners from Circle Projects, a local arts organisation, developed the approach they call 'Eye to eye' as a way of enabling children to explore their relationships in a creative and positive way and develop new strategies to tackle problems of bullying.

Three junior schools invited Circle Projects to develop work based around 'Eye to eye' with their Year 6 classes over the course of two terms.[11] It was seen as a way of helping to ease the children's transition from primary to secondary education, and also as an opportunity to create better relationships between the feeder schools and the local secondary school, Chillwell Comprehensive. As part of the project students from Chillwell were invited to get involved. This served a dual function, encouraging the juniors to obtain a clearer picture of life in the comprehensive school through their contact with the students, thus lessening their fears, and offering the secondary students a chance to exercise their responsibility and empathise with the concerns of the younger children. ■

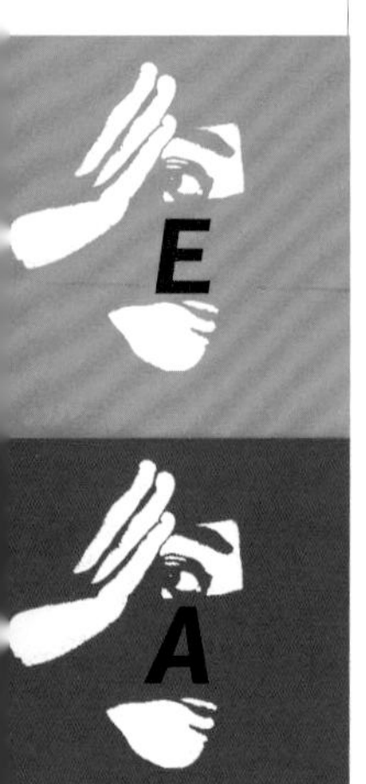

E

A

'Eye to eye' activities

This project involves a great deal of preparation and groundwork and the images shown are part of a drama-based activity created by children as they reflected on what they had learnt and experienced throughout their two terms working on 'Eye to eye'. Therefore you will

John Clifford Primary School

PSHE and RE

need to have spent a considerable time discussing with the children issues such as identity, fear and anxiety, co-operation, prejudice and tolerance, and different forms of bullying, drawing on their own experiences, ideas and feelings before attempting the following activities. See art chapter for further details.

- Divide the class into groups of five or six and ask group members to delegate roles amongst them. They should understand that they will be creating a scene using drama, with the addition of light and colour projection, that reflects the work they have already done around bullying. Their roles will range from the creation of puppets and props to narration, storyboarding, acting, direction and organisation. One member from each group should also take the role of photographer to document the completed scene. By having specific roles each child's strengths are then valued and drawn on by the group as a whole.

John Clifford Primary School

- The groups should spend time planning, creating and presenting their scene. Each could be given storyboard sheets to sketch their ideas, sequence them and make notes. It is important that the children understand that they will be using symbolic representations rather than literal or stereotypical depictions of their ideas. For instance a character who bullies may be represented as a tiger who then turns into a bird as she finds better ways of relating to others.
- While the children are planning you will need to stretch a large white sheet between two uprights to act as a shadow screen for the children to perform behind. The OHP or slide projector is then positioned behind the screen, and by performing between the two the children will be seen as shadows or silhouettes.
- Once each group has planned their scene an order needs to be decided on for presentation. In Nottingham there was a limit of three minutes for presentation of each finished piece, therefore the children needed to storyboard their ideas tightly. Each scene should then be documented by the child allocated as photographer from the appropriate group, with the focus on recording visually striking or important moments. ■

- A large space to work in
- Storyboard sheets for planning
- OHP, acetate, coloured gels, OHP pens, materials for cut-outs
- Slide projector and slide mounts for gels and other materials
- Large white sheet stretched between two uprights for the shadow screen
- 35mm camera and colour print or slide film to document the projections or a video camera

'Alternative images'

Social stereotypes reinforce perceptions of gender roles and affect children's learning. This image is one of a series of four posters that have been produced with children at Stroud Green Junior school.[12] The starting point was to ask the children simple questions such as: 'What is a job?' and 'What would you like to be when you grow up?'. Although girls and boys may now have similar career expectations their motives have remained gender specific. An example is two children who had the same aspiration: to be a vet; the girl's reason was 'because I would like to help animals get better' and the boy's 'because I am interested in medicine'.

In this activity the image works against the text in order to avoid reinforcing existing stereotypes and to avoid the supply of simple answers to complex questions. Each question should lead to further questions, most importantly asking: Why? These activities allow the teacher to address the needs of PSHE and RE by making effective intervention through active discussion, exploring messages and challenging stereotyping. ■

'Alternative images' discussion points

The following questions and statements have been raised by children themselves in relation to the accompanying image.

- Do you agree with the statement on the poster? Is it true or false? Why?
- Can women be doctors, judges, train drivers? Why do you think that is?
- Name some jobs where women are usually in charge.
- What do you think about the following statements?
  - 'Women have to fight harder to get jobs'
  - 'A man can be a librarian and a woman can be a mechanic'
  - 'Men think they are the bread-winners. Men don't like children; women are better, more used to children. Men can't stand crying children'
  - 'I think that both men and women should have equal jobs and they should both stay at home and look after house and family, not just the women' ■

Stroud Green Infants School

Bidwell Brook Special School

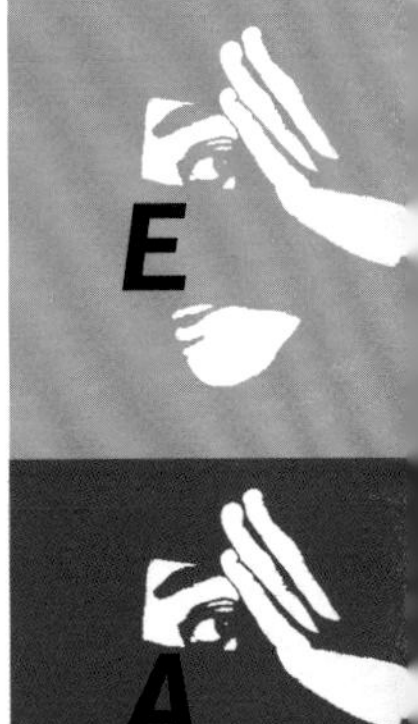

'Alternative images' activities

- Look at visual representations of women and girls in magazines, advertising and the media. Make two separate collections, one showing stereotyped images and the other alternative images.
- Ask the children to take portraits of each other and then to select identities for themselves using found images or their own drawings, showing who they would like to be when they grow up. Superimpose their heads on to their chosen body. Ask the children to comment on their choices. Children at Bidwell Brook Special School, Devon, used computers to create new identities for themselves.[13]
- Ask the class if either of their parents has unusual or unexpected jobs. Some parents could then be contacted and asked to come and talk about their jobs at school.
- Rewrite or invert traditional stories, developing different alternative female roles.
- Ask the children to explore the role of the opposite sex by engaging with drama, role-play and creative writing. ■

Resources

- Poster pack *Alternative Images: Issues of Gender* (see bibliography) or suitable images for initiating discussion

Project credits

1. 'Ourselves': Lee Brigg First School, West Yorkshire. Reception and Key Stage 1.
   Sarah Mumford, advisory teacher and Joan Cook, class teacher
2. 'Hospital project': Part 1: Chelsea and Westminster Children's Hospital School, London.
   The Photographers' Gallery, London, Joy Gregory, photographer, and Rod Hutchinson, teacher
3. 'I dream of being': Part 1: Camp JMI School, Hertfordshire. Key Stage 2.
   Kim Walden, animateur, Sarah Jones, photographer and Sarah Thurley, class teacher
4. 'Clothes and stories': Londonmeed Primary School, West Sussex. Key Stage 1.
   Jenny Fox, advisory teacher and Joyce Wright, class teacher
5. 'I dream of being': Part 2: Camp JMI School, Hertfordshire. Key Stage 2.
   Kim Walden, animateur, Sarah Jones, photographer and Sarah Thurley, class teacher
6. 'Light': Mount Pleasant Junior School, Southampton. Key Stage 2.
   Mount Pleasant Media Workshop, Helen Cooksey and Liz Filer, class teachers, Marcus Cole, artist
7. 'Digital identities': Thomas Jones Primary School, London. Key Stage 2.
   The Photographers' Gallery, London, Fiona Bailey, photographer, Jane Brake, advisory teacher, Joy Smith and Kath Griffiths, class teachers
8. 'Hospital project:' Part 2: The Chelsea and Westminster Children's Hospital School at the Royal Brompton Heart and Lung Hospital Site, London.
   The Photographers' Gallery, London, Alistair Raphael, photographer, and Sarah Cliff, teacher
9. 'Home lives': Snowsfields Primary School, London. Key Stage 2.
   Blackfriars Photography Project, London, Kamina Walton, photographer and Jasmine Jayham, class teacher
10. 'Light': Mount Pleasant Junior School, Southampton. Key Stage 2.
    Mount Pleasant Media Workshop, Southampton, Helen Cooksey and Liz Filer, class teachers, Marcus Cole, artist
11. 'Eye to eye – the bullying project': John Clifford Primary School and Chillwell Comprehensive, Nottingham. Key Stage 2.
    Circle Projects, Jo Solomon, Daniel Saul, Karen Rew and Kay Brown.
12. 'Alternative images': Stroud Green Infants School, London. Key Stages 1 and 2.
    Middlesex University, Victoria de Rijke, senior lecturer, and Geoffrey Cox, photographer.
13. 'Judge': Bidwell Brook Special School, Devon. Key Stage 2.
    Julia Bond, head of lower school and creative arts. ■

Where do I live?

Geography

Where do we live?

Where do I live?

Geography at Key Stages 1 and 2 is intended to increase children's awareness of their immediate surroundings while also introducing them to the concept of the world beyond and their place within it.

Taking and looking at photographs in geography can encourage and develop both general enquiry skills such as observation, recording and analysing evidence, and specific geographical skills of fieldwork, scale in mapping and learning to read photographs for information. Working in this medium can help to develop children's understanding of scale in relation to physical space, maps and plans, and also help them make comparisons between the physical and human features of one place and another. Observational skills are of key importance as they equip children first to understand their immediate surroundings, and then to understand the world beyond. By using a viewfinder children develop a structured way of looking, their observation is heightened and they are encouraged to engage actively in investigation.

It has been asserted that geography is always imagined before it is seen and mapped. At Key Stage 1 the exploration of place is not restricted to the realm of the real – imaginary places or fictional landscapes can be constructed through various photographic practices. The visualisation of make-believe places can allow children's imaginations to transport them beyond the classroom, enabling them to start playfully exploring questions that form the basis for geographical vocabulary, for example: What/where is it? How did it get like this? Is it hot or cold?

At both Key Stages, cameras enable children, when learning about their locality, to look afresh at their familiar surroundings and gather geographical information, while taking photographs can enable them to frame their own personal statements and become more fully involved in a project. When taking cameras home these photographs can also portray personal environments which are not documented anywhere else.

For a long time teachers have used photographic illustrations as a way of bringing information about the world into the classroom, and in this way have treated them as a form of observation. The project examples set out in this chapter seek not only to demonstrate how photography can play a more central role in the delivery of the subject, but also to teach children that a photograph derives its meaning in part from its function, and is not necessarily a 'window on the world'. By creating their own images and taking full control of the picture-making process children can begin to understand this. ■

Aims

- To help children investigate and understand their immediate surroundings, to develop an awareness of the world and their place within it, and to understand that the world extends beyond their own locality, both within and outside the United Kingdom.
- To help children to develop skills in observation, exploration, questioning, analysis, recording and communication.
- To help children understand that photographs are not just 'windows on the world' but are taken from a specific point of view to convey particular meanings.

My home

'Houses and homes'

Taking as a starting point the class topic 'Houses and homes' this project aimed to provide an opportunity for children at William Tyndale Primary School, London, to become involved in using photography and mixed media to explore the built environment in which they were growing up.[1] The project was co-ordinated by the education department at The Photographers' Gallery, London, and a photographer worked in collaboration with staff at the school. It enabled children to investigate their surroundings actively, encouraging them to look in detail at a range of different buildings, houses, homes and ways of life from a variety of cultural and social perspectives.

The children collected and assembled their own and found photographs. They combined them with drawings, paintings and photocopies, all of which were collaged together and pasted on to a house-shaped framework, made by a parent, to form a huge, and visually stunning, three-dimensional 'photo-sculpture' house. ■

'Houses and homes' activities

- Begin by showing the class a range of images of interiors and exteriors of buildings from around the world. Discussion could focus on similarities and differences between local buildings the children are familiar with and those from other countries and cultures that may be unfamiliar to them. Questions such as: 'What are these buildings used for?' and 'What materials have been used to construct them?' will encourage the children to look more carefully at the images.
- Ask each child to investigate their surroundings actively, looking through a viewfinder, and to choose an area to draw that they find interesting. This should be a small area in space, such as a section of wall with a picture on it, a door handle, or an unusual feature in the room. This is partly to make the drawing activity more manageable, but also to allow for the different elements to be brought together to make a group collage.
- Once the drawings are complete they can be cut out and the children can decide where each one should be positioned in relation to the next, depending on the geographical space represented. They can then be pasted together on a large piece of card.
- The next stage is to use photographs to document the school (from both inside and out), the immediate locality and the children's homes. At this point the class could be divided into groups and each group could be allocated a different area to work on. Again

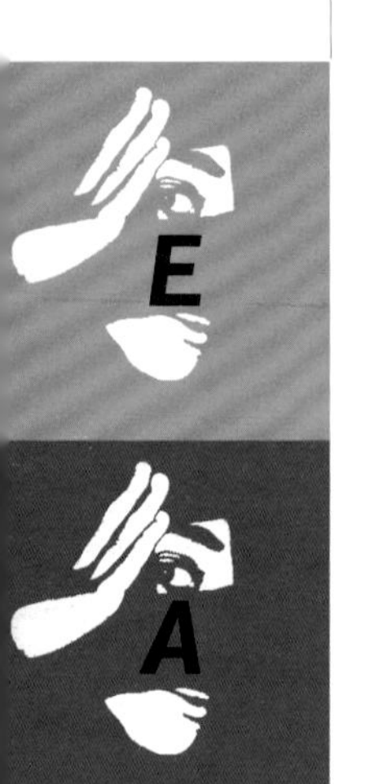

they could focus on details, or on a more general representation of the place or space they are documenting. Each group could be allocated a roll of film between them and photographs could be planned on paper before they are actually taken to avoid wastage.

- The group taking cameras home could be given a set of criteria for the photographs they should take and the number they take could be limited, maybe to six each. Providing a set of guidelines for the photographs, such as the ones below, might be helpful:
  a) your home in its setting, or the approach to your front door if that is easier
  b) your favourite place within the home
  c) your favourite toy or possession
  d) your favourite food that you eat at home
  e) your favourite time of day
  f) your favourite view, either inside or out of a window
  By using cameras to record their personal environment children are creating a unique form of geographic documentation.

William Tyndale Primary School

- Once all the photographs have been taken and the films processed the images can be spread out on tables and the children can group them in one of a number of ways: in relation to geographic areas within the locality; into themes, such as windows, doorways or stairs; or into interior and exterior locations. In any of these groupings the class can separate those photographs that they are happy with from those that they feel are unsuccessful, however, when doing this they should be fully aware of their reasons.
- Key images can be selected from each group, then enlarged on the photocopier and hand coloured, using wax crayons or ink washes. Again, at this point the class could be working in groups with some children colouring, some pasting images to the backing panels or card, and some collecting found images from magazines to mix with their own. At William Tyndale the photographs were pasted on to backing board with spaces between each one and these spaces

William Tyndale Primary School

Resources

- Images of buildings, both interiors and exteriors, from around the world
- Plastic slide mounts or card viewfinders
- Drawing materials, scissors, glue sticks and card
- 35mm camera (with built-in flash for home photos) and colour print films
- Structure, display boards or thick card to mount finished work on
- A suitable space for installation of the work

were then painted by the children, creating a framework for their images. The groups can be rotated to give variety to the activities.

- At William Tyndale the work was collaged together to create a three-dimensional structure, with an exterior and an interior, which was put up in the classroom. However, if you decide this is too complicated, the children's images could be displayed on a two-dimensional surface such as a display board or room divider, one side for the exterior and the other for the interior. ■

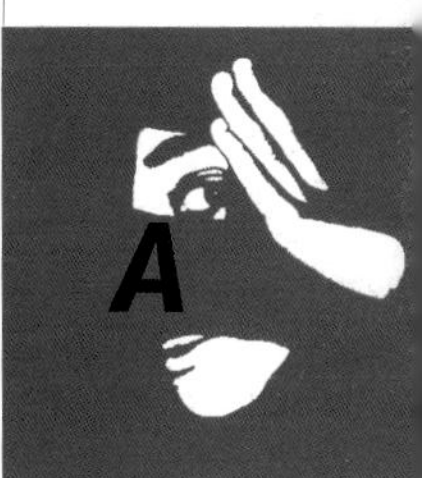

William Tyndale Primary School

Further activities

- Children at William Tyndale concentrated on built structures in the locality but work could be extended to include open spaces, such as gardens or parks, and the resulting images combined for the final presentation.
- Other elements such as photocopies of local maps could be incorporated into the final display. ■

Imaginary places

'Children representing themselves'

'Children representing themselves' was a photographic project co-ordinated by Watershed Media Centre, Bristol, that involved a photographer in residence working over a period of two months in two local schools: with a Year 6 class at May Park Primary, and with a group of Year 3 children at The Park Primary.[2] Although this project was originally carried out with Key Stage 2 children, it has been adapted in this context for Key Stage 1. The children were given the opportunity to explore childhood from their own point of view, while taking full control of the picture-making process.

Using magazines, holiday brochures, books and newspapers as source material, part of the project involved the children entering the realms of fantasy by placing their own cut-out portraits within an environment of their choosing. The choices of location made were diverse – one child brought in a plastic table mat depicting a Chinese water garden scene that she wanted to enter, while another, an avid *Star Trek* watcher, placed himself in a desert landscape, imagining that he had just been 'transported' there. As well as developing the children's understanding of image construction by having the chance to appear in fantastic places, the project stimulated them to imagine what it might be like being in those places. In this way they learnt to ask questions of their surroundings and in their responses used geographical terms and vocabulary to describe a sense of place. ■

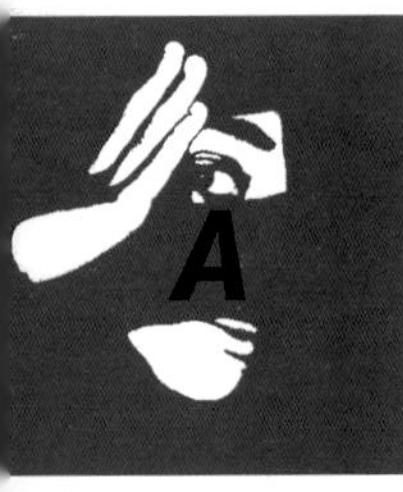

'Children representing themselves' activities

- Ask the children to look through a range of resources to find a location or environment that they would like to place themselves within. This research could take place at school or at home and obviously the more resources available the greater opportunity the children will have of finding their ideal location. If they choose an image from a book this could be photocopied and hand coloured, or, if they prefer, they could create their own setting using drawing or painting, or by combining their own art work with a found image.
- Ask the children, working in pairs, to photograph their partner in a way that will relate to the environment that they are going to place themselves within. This will involve discussion with their partner as

to exactly where they will place themselves and how they want to be photographed, for example, how much of the body should be visible, in which direction should they be looking and what kind of body position might they adopt.

- Once the film has been processed each child should cut out their portrait and place it within their chosen environment. They could then write about how they might feel in this new environment – whether it is hot or cold, whether they feel relaxed or maybe frightened, the sounds they might hear and the smells they might detect. ■

Alliya Nayeem/May Park Primary School

Jamie Pillinger/The Park Primary School

Resources

- Wide range of image resources for the children to select their location from
- 35mm camera and colour print film

A place for me

'Portraits in the landscape'

In collaboration with The Photographers' Gallery, London and Richard Wilson Arts Centre, Nantlle, North Wales, Key Stage 2 children at a small rural primary school worked with a photgrapher in residence and used photography to picture themselves within their immediate environment.

Ysgol Baladeulyn School, 'Between Two Lakes', is situated at the foot of Snowdon and is surrounded by mountains close to the coast at Caernarfon.[3] The area was once known for its prosperous slate quarry industry. These quarries are now closed and the area has suffered great economic hardship. The school has two classes, one for each Key Stage, which together have a total of 48 children, all of whom are Welsh-speaking. Through the medium of photography the children were given the opportunity to explore their environment and the places where they play, position themselves within those surroundings and dress up in clothes associated with play, for example, fancy dress or masks. These 'environmental portraits' show a child's interpretation of their surroundings and their place within it. The children also wrote poems, inspired by their photographs, describing how certain places made them feel and the associations they had with them, providing lyrical descriptions of their lives, their villages, the mountains and the sea. ■

Sion Williams/Ysgol Baladeulyn School

Kirsty Tivers/Ysgol Baladeulyn School

Baladeulyn Bridge
Rushing to the bridge
Looking,
Hearing,
Water flowing
From the Lake.

Then
Looking
Straight up
Behold! Seeing! Noticing!
Snowdon with the snow on top,
Thinking how cold winter is.

Bont Baladeulyn
Rhedeg at y bont
Gweld,
Clywed,
Dwr yn llifo
O'r llyn.

Yna
Edrych
yn syth i fyny
Gweld! Synnu! Sylwi!
Ar yr Wyddfa gyda'r eira,
Meddwl, pa mor oer yw'r gaeaf.

Alaw Roberts

'Portraits in the landscape' activities

- Ask the children to think about the places where they play in the local community and then to create maps showing where these places are in relation to their homes or the school.
- Ask the children, as a class, questions about what they do in these places, the kind of games they play, whether they play alone or with friends or siblings, and whether it is imaginative or another kind of play. They could then be encouraged to write individual accounts of the activities they engage in while in these places.
- The next stage is to organise visits to the individual sites, or, if this is unfeasible, to give the children a camera that they can take home with them for a day or two to photograph their chosen play space. Disposable cameras can be useful for sending home although they do work out more expensive than re-usable cameras in the long-term.
- As with the class in Wales the children could then write poems inspired by their photographs. ■

Resources

- 35mm camera or disposable cameras
- Colour or black and white film
- Costumes or toys for individual photos if applicable

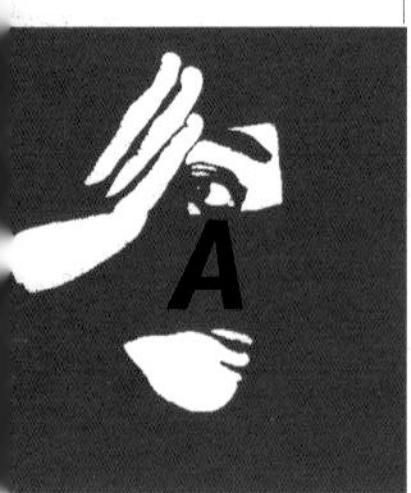

Re-presenting my locality

'An alien environment'

As part of the collaborative project 'Myself and my environment', between the Photographers' Gallery and Chelsea and Westminster Children's Hospital, London, children attending the Royal Brompton Heart and Lung Hospital school site used photography to represent the hospital environment from unusual points of view.[4] The intention was to encourage the children to see their surroundings in a different way, and to locate those surroundings in relation to their home environments. Viewfinders were used as a starting point to frame the children's vision and abstract what they could see. Sitting in a circle they used these frames to look at details around them, whether related to themselves, others in the circle or the physical space. A camera was then passed around and each child took a photograph. The children then went on to take further photographs of isolated details of objects, people or places that existed within the hospital schoolroom and the ward.

This project had to be completed in one-half day session as the children participating often stayed at the hospital only long enough to take part on one occasion. For this reason Polaroid slide film was used to provide instant results. There was discussion during the workshop about reproducing the images as postcards that could be sent to the children's friends or family to emphasise further the idea of their surroundings being different or 'alien'. The results show a fascinating document of a hospital environment from a child's point of view. ■

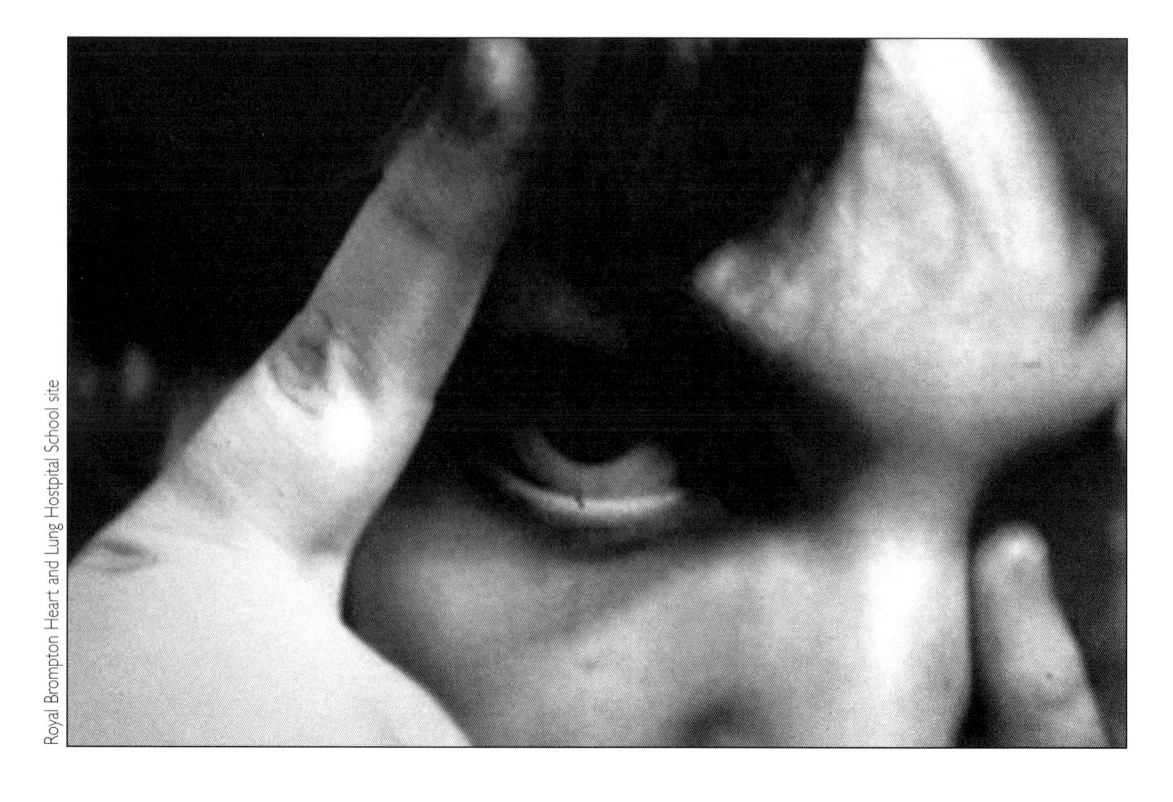

Royal Brompton Heart and Lung Hostpital School site

'An alien environment' activities

- Ask the children to imagine that they have just arrived in their classroom from another planet. Everything will be completely different to their own world so they have to try and imagine that they are seeing their surroundings for the first time. Give each child a viewfinder and send them off to explore the environment very carefully, looking closely to observe the texture, colour, etc. of each thing they come across. At the Royal Brompton children used their viewfinders to explore the schoolroom and the children's ward as well as the objects and equipment there.
- Once they have looked around in detail ask them to choose an area that they find particularly interesting and take a number of photographs. These could be of something specific taken from a variety of angles, or of a number of things that appear in this one small area.
- When the film has been processed spread the photographs out on the tables and see if the class can identify the content of each photograph.
- Selected individual prints could then be mounted on card to strengthen them and they could be treated as postcards. Messages describing this 'alien' environment could be written on the back to other children in the school or to parents. ■

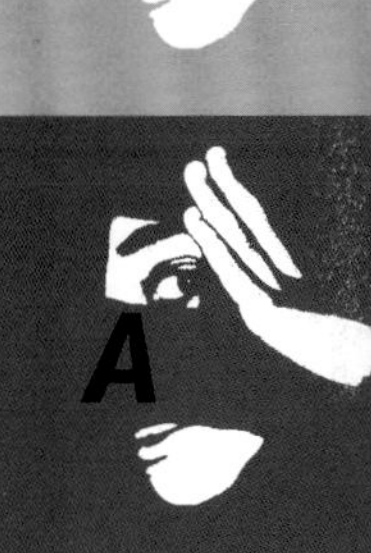

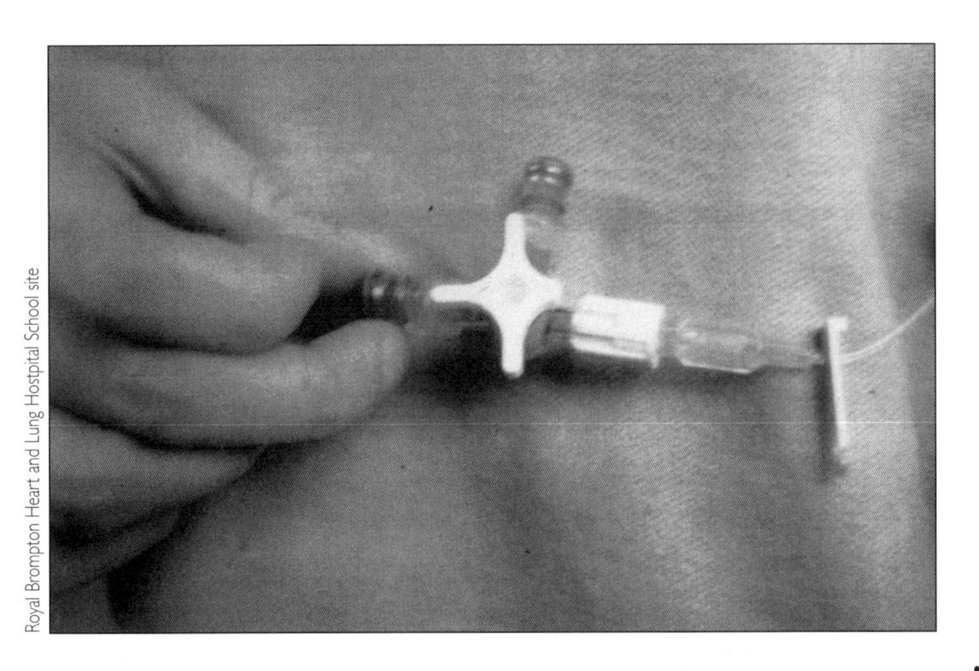

Royal Brompton Heart and Lung Hostpital School site

Resources

- Plastic or card viewfinders
- 35mm camera with a close-up filter or lens and colour print film
- Card for backing photographs and writing materials

'Give us a clue'

At Barton Hill Junior School, Bristol, a class studying the local environment worked with a photographer, commissioned by Barton Hill Photography Project, to create an interactive display.[5] The aim of the project was for each child to photograph a chosen place from two points of view – one as a straightforward document of that place and the other as a close-up of a small area or detail within that place. The children were also involved in quite complex language work as they had to produce a written clue for their close-up photograph that would help those playing the game of matching it to its partner image.

Work began with discussion about where individual children lived, played and shopped, and these places where plotted on a local map. They were then asked about any recent changes that had occurred in the local area, and went on to study historical photographs to learn of changes that had taken place over the decades. Barton Hill is a close-knit community and many families have lived there for generations, therefore questionnaires were also sent home to the children's parents with the intention of asking similar questions of an older generation. ■

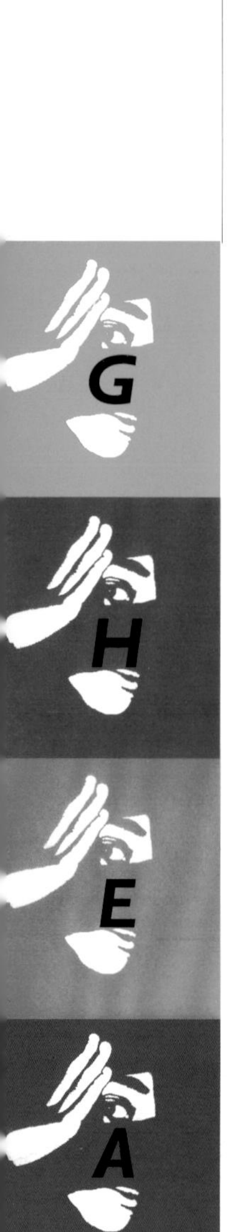

'Give us a clue' activities

- Working with children in groups or as a whole class begin by talking to them about the local area in relation to where they live, play, shop, etc.
- Explain to the class that they are going to create a game that involves the players matching up two photographs – one showing a place clearly and the other just showing a very small part of that place. The class should then be divided into groups. The children should plan where they are going to take their photographs and keep the decision secret from the other groups. If working in this way it will be necessary to enrol the help of a general assistant, and possibly a parent, to enable one group to go out into the community at a time.
- At Barton Hill each child then took two photographs – one showing the clear view and one of the close-up. When taking the close-up the children should think carefully about what they are including and excluding in the photograph. The framing they choose should include information that is also visible in their other image in order to provide a visual clue.
- They must then devise captions to accompany the two photographs. The caption for the close-up should act as a written clue to the visual clue provided in the close-up image. The caption to accompany their other image should explain why they chose to photograph that place. This can be a time-consuming activity and, depending on the age and ability of the class, children may need individual help to complete the exercise successfully. Once finished,

Barton Hill Junior School

A

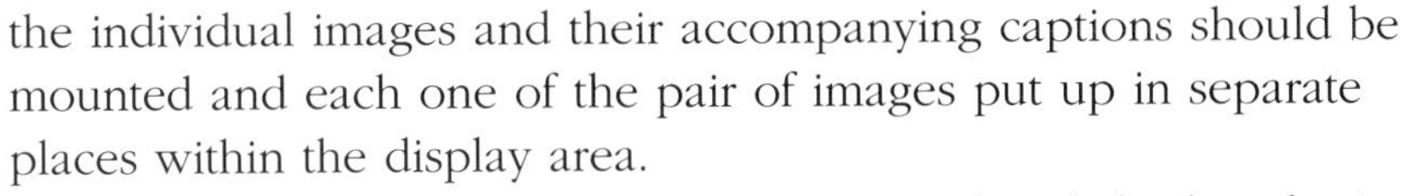

the individual images and their accompanying captions should be mounted and each one of the pair of images put up in separate places within the display area.

- Once all the photographs have been mounted and displayed, pieces of cotton or thread can be hung directly above or beneath the close-up photographs and their clues. The game is to attach the free end of the thread to the photograph that it links up with. If the groups have been kept separate from one another throughout the whole activity the children can try and solve the clues created by those in other groups. Other classes can then be invited in to try and match all the pairs of photographs together. ■

Resources

- Old photographs of the local area
- A map that can be marked with the children's homes, etc.
- 35mm camera (with close-up facility or lens) and colour print films
- Computer to type up captions
- Backing paper for mounting and thread and pins for display

Barton Hill Junior School

My environment

'Environmental advertising'

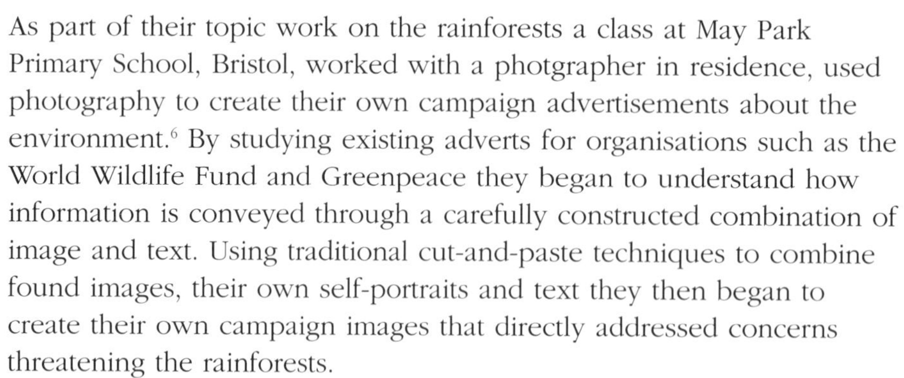

As part of their topic work on the rainforests a class at May Park Primary School, Bristol, worked with a photgrapher in residence, used photography to create their own campaign advertisements about the environment.[6] By studying existing adverts for organisations such as the World Wildlife Fund and Greenpeace they began to understand how information is conveyed through a carefully constructed combination of image and text. Using traditional cut-and-paste techniques to combine found images, their own self-portraits and text they then began to create their own campaign images that directly addressed concerns threatening the rainforests.

Having experimented with montage techniques and the use of image and text, the children went on to work in groups to create photo-stories relating to a variety of environmental threats. Once they had decided on an issue to base their story around they used storyboard sheets to plan the narrative and to sequence their images. Again they worked with their own photographs, found images, drawings and photocopies from books; by combining them they created not only successful narrative sequences but groupwork that clearly presented what they had learnt of issues threatening the environment. ■

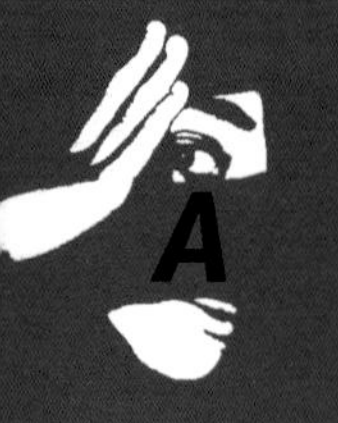

'Environmental advertising' activities

- Collect together a range of advertisements from newspapers and magazines, articles about environmental issues and leaflets produced by environmental organisations. Organisations such as those mentioned above are usually happy to provide information to schools and will send their recent campaign material or information packs on request. The class should look at the images and accompanying text used by different organisations and then be asked about the similarities or differences they have noticed in the campaigns and whether they think the organisations manage to put their messages across effectively.
- Focusing on the class topic, whether it is about the rainforests or another environmental issue, ask the children to decide independently on an issue that they want to produce a campaign image for. Once they have decided on this they can then look through a range of resource material for an image to act as a background. The selected material can then be photocopied.

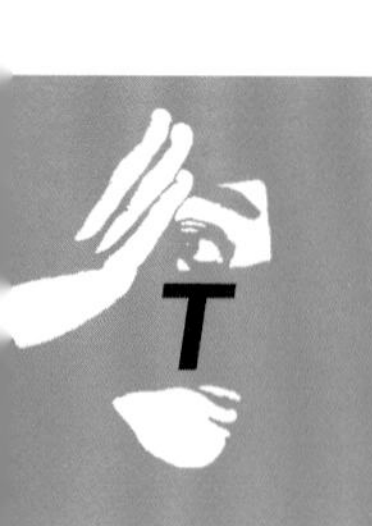

Geography

- The next step is to ask the children to work in pairs and take a photograph of their partner. This will be cut out and inserted into their selected background, therefore if care is taken in the planning of these portraits they will be more effective when combined with the found image. Things that should be taken into consideration are the children's facial expressions, where they are looking, their body positions and which direction they are facing.
- Once the film has been processed each child can cut out their portrait and paste it on to their background which can then be hand coloured with inks or coloured pencils. Captions can then be created to accompany their image.

Sheldon Ellis/May Park Primary School

Resources

- Range of images and leaflets about environmental issues
- Books, magazines, etc. to select backgrounds from
- 35mm camera and colour print films
- Inks and/or coloured pencils
- Access to a photocopier
- Storyboard sheets
- Computer to generate text

- To take the project a stage further divide the class into groups and give each one a storyboard sheet. Ask the children to focus on an environmental topic and create a story about it. Again, they can work with a combination of their own photographs, found images, drawing and text to present their photo-story. At May Park the children were limited to a maximum of eight images for their photo-stories. This meant they had to be concise about the information that they needed to put across and had to devise effective ways of representing their ideas. ■

Esther Bartlett, Sian Bartlett, Sameena Kausar and Charleene Nelson/May Park Primary School

Representing my world

'Bias and viewpoint'

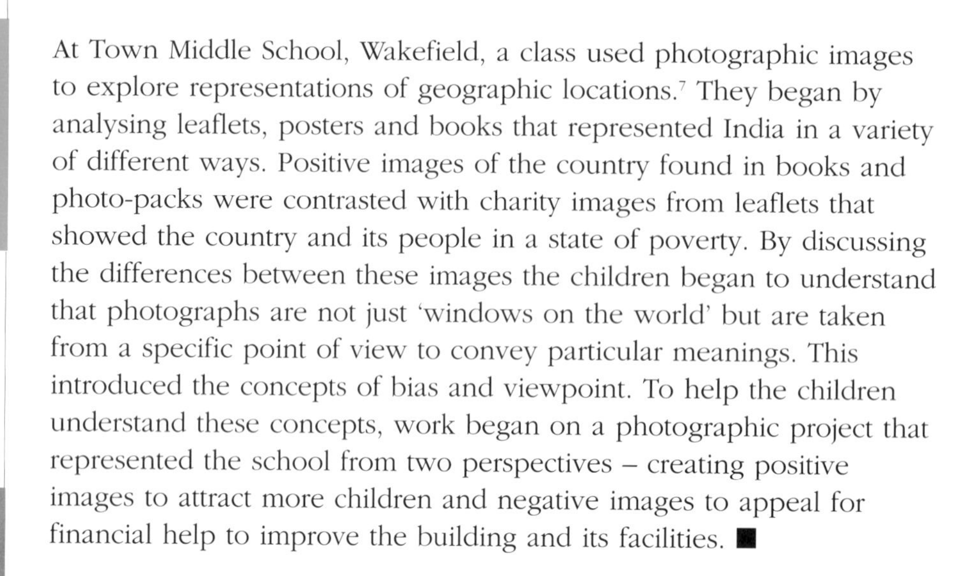

At Town Middle School, Wakefield, a class used photographic images to explore representations of geographic locations.[7] They began by analysing leaflets, posters and books that represented India in a variety of different ways. Positive images of the country found in books and photo-packs were contrasted with charity images from leaflets that showed the country and its people in a state of poverty. By discussing the differences between these images the children began to understand that photographs are not just 'windows on the world' but are taken from a specific point of view to convey particular meanings. This introduced the concepts of bias and viewpoint. To help the children understand these concepts, work began on a photographic project that represented the school from two perspectives – creating positive images to attract more children and negative images to appeal for financial help to improve the building and its facilities. ■

'Bias and viewpoint' activities

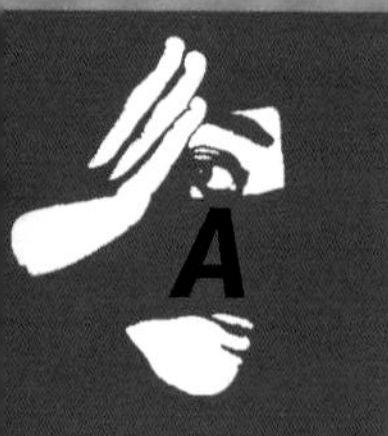

- Gather together a range of images from books, leaflets, posters, etc. representing a country, such as India, from different perspectives. Compile a list of questions about the content of the images. Ask the children to answer these questions either working in pairs on paper, or as a class through general discussion.
- Once this activity has been completed divide the class into groups and ask them to think about one positive and one negative image that they could produce of their school for use on a poster or leaflet. They could then sketch their ideas and make notes about the captions that could accompany their images.
- Each group should then take their photographs, giving thought to the camera angle, distance and what can be seen in the background and foreground of their photographs. While waiting for the film to be processed they can be planning the layout for their leaflets or posters, maybe producing text on the computer.
- When the photographs are ready the children can sort them into successful and unsuccessful results. In this way they are going through a similar process to that undertaken by picture editors, ending up with the most suitable images for the job. Photographs and text can then be combined to produce the finished images.
- Each group could then present their work to the rest of the class which could comment on how successful they feel the work has been in presenting a positive or negative image of the school. Individual groups could then evaluate their own work. ■

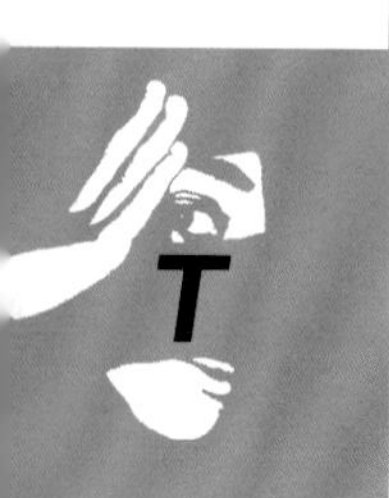

Town Middle School

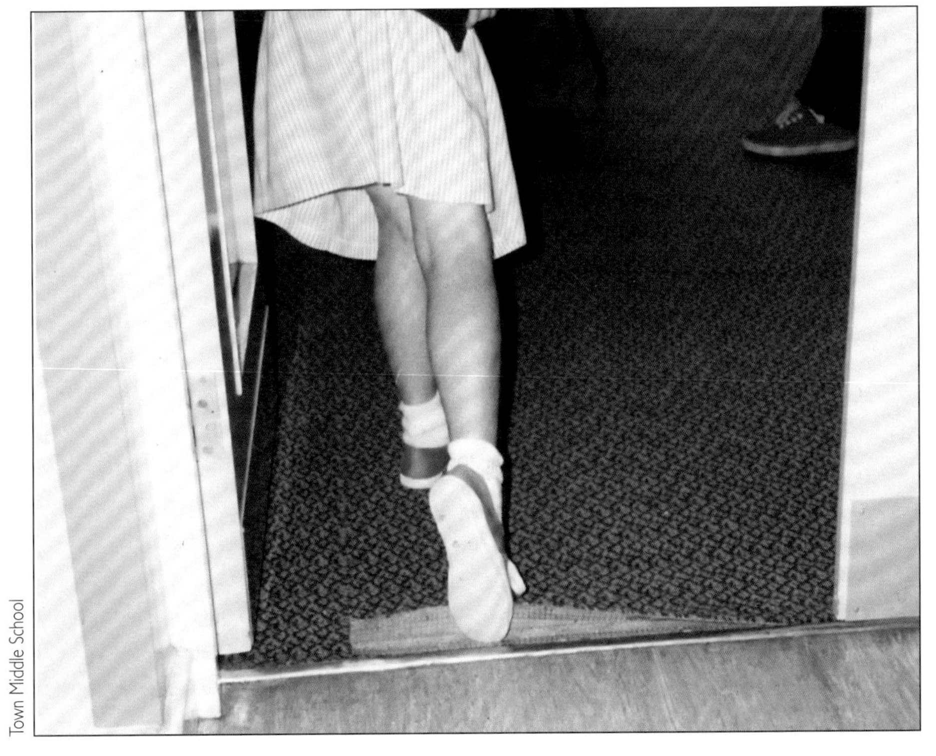

Town Middle School

Resources

- Leaflets, posters and books representing a country and its people
- 35mm camera and colour print film
- Computer for text production
- Paper or card, colour pencils, scissors and glue stick for final presentation

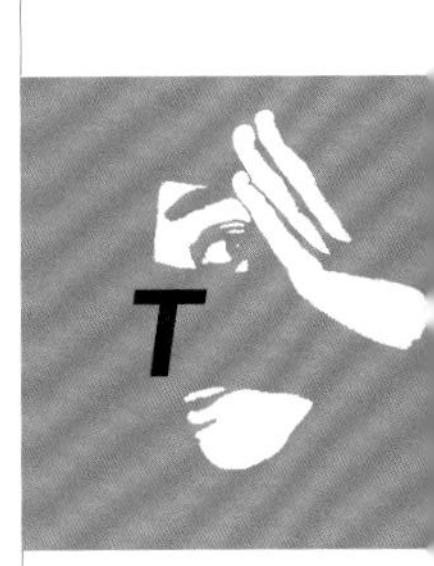

Project credits

1. 'Houses and homes': William Tyndale Primary School, London, Key Stage 1.
   The Photographers' Gallery, London, Shona Illingworth, artist and Anne Chowne and Rebecca Stone, class teachers
2. 'Children representing themselves': May Park Primary and The Park Primary School, Bristol, Key Stage 2.
   Watershed Media Centre, Bristol, Kamina Walton, photographer, Georgia Taylor and Sarah Shaw, class teachers
3. 'Portraits in the landscape': Ysgol Baladeulyn School, North Wales, Key Stages 1 and 2.
   The Photographers' Gallery, London, Richard Wilson Arts Centre, Nantlle, North Wales, Jan Chipps, photographer and Susan Jane Owen, class teacher
4. 'An alien environment': The Chelsea and Westminster Children's Hospital School at the Royal Brompton Heart and Lung Hospital site, London.
   The Photographers' Gallery, London, Alistair Raphael, photographer and Sarah Cliff, teacher
5. 'Give us a clue': Barton Hill Junior School, Bristol, Key Stage 2.
   Barton Hill Photography Project, Bristol, Kamina Walton, photographer and Heather Glanville, class teacher
6. 'Advertising and the environment': May Park Primary School, Bristol, Key Stage 2.
   Kamina Walton, photographer and Louisa Wilson, class teacher
7. 'Bias and viewpoint': Town Middle School, Wakefield, Key Stage 2.
   Sarah Mumford, advisory teacher and Mrs Mallinski, class teacher ■

Geography planning grid

Key Stage	Project	Area of study
1	Houses and homes	1ab 2 3bf
1	Children representing themselves	1b 3adf
1	Portraits in the landscape	1ab 2 3bdf
1	An alien environment	1a 3b
2	Give us a clue	1ab 2abc 3bc 4 5d
2	Environmental advertising	3e 10ab
2	Bias and viewpoint	1a 2abc 3ef 4 5a

How did I live?

History

How did we live?

How did I live?

Aims

- To give children the opportunity to develop an awareness of the past and the ways in which it is different from the present.
- To develop children's skills in acquiring knowledge about the past and in using a chronological framework.
- To help children understand that historical events can be represented in different ways, and that these representations can affect the interpretation of an event.
- To develop children's ability to express themselves clearly in written and visual work and through speech, and to develop their reading skills.
- To give children appropriate opportunities to develop and apply an information technology capability to the study of history.

This chapter draws on projects that use a variety of photographic approaches and techniques as a key method for teaching history at Key Stages 1 and 2. They involve the study of personal family history, exploration of local history, making direct use and comparisons between the past and the present, and questioning representations of particular historical events, asking: whose history is this?

In order to understand the world as as it is today and society children must understand certain events that have happened in the past. To introduce the basic concepts of history at Key Stage 1 the areas of study begin with familiar events, people and places in the present and move to everyday life in the past. Photographs from family albums can form the basis for reminiscences, memories and testimonies to ways of life which are fast disappearing. By charting familiar changes in their own lives children are able to grasp the fundamental concept of the past and this provides a good starting point for the study of the subject. Exercises in sequencing photographs will demonstrate chronology and engender the need for words and phrases describing the passing of time; personal time-lines are one accessible way of introducing these concepts to children.

As in other subjects, photographic practice in history can develop children's study skills, their critical thought, communication and interpersonal skills. At Key Stage 2 children should be developing their research techniques and their ability to make links both within and across time periods, with the focus on important historical events in the history of the UK and elements of history from other parts of the world. Historical events can be represented in different ways and these representations can affect the interpretation of an event. Photographs from family albums can introduce the idea that interpretations of history can differ as a child relays the memory of an experience as opposed to the photographic representation of the event.

The range of photographic approaches described here can be applied at any stage of the child's learning, enabling them to communicate historical knowledge effectively in a variety of different ways. One of the main intentions of these projects is to use the medium of photography and photographic reconstruction as a way of bringing alive the past, thereby motivating and exciting children's interest in the subject. ■

My family album

'Family albums'

At Bournhall JMI School, Hertfordshire, a Channel 4 series 'Beyond the family album' and the accompanying booklet, *The Family Album*, were the starting point for a classroom project.[1] Although this project was originally carried out with Key Stage 2 children, it has been adapted in this context for Key Stage 1. Work began through class discussions about photographs and children developed a list of places where photographs might be found within the home. They made a separate list of anywhere else they may have seen them, for example, on lunch boxes or pencil cases. Children were asked whether one particular person in the family tended to take photographs or whether the activity was shared, who or what appeared most frequently in the images and who usually put the photographs in the family album. The children then looked at the different types of photography that might be found in the family album, focusing on those that they had direct experience of, such as baby photos, the school photograph, holiday snaps and wedding pictures. Comparisons were made between images that might be taken today and those that might have been taken in the past, and discussion led to more general questions about the function of photography in our lives.

Images from the family album are readily available and can provide a starting point for discussion about the multicultural make-up of a school and the range of cultural backgrounds from which children might come. Photographs can also serve as a bridge between home and school for children in their early school years. ■

'Family albums' activities

- Ask the children to bring in a selection of baby photographs from home. It may be an idea to send a letter home explaining the project to parents and offering to photocopy images and return them immediately if they are concerned about them being damaged. If parents are unwilling for album photographs to be used postcards or images from magazines can be substituted.
- Encourage the children to 'read' their images, first by describing what they can see and second by interpreting what they think is happening in the photograph. Discussion can then focus on how conventions for baby photography have changed. For many children today their first photographic portrait may be an ultrasound image taken of the unborn foetus as early as sixteen weeks. Some of the oldest examples of baby photography are from the Victorian times when child mortality was high and many bereaved parents

had photographs taken of their dead children for remembrance.

- By photocopying their images the children can begin to collate their own photograph album which also includes their written work.
- The next stage could be to look at school photographs, again asking questions such as, what kind of photographs are taken by a school photographer and how these representations of children have changed over the years. ■

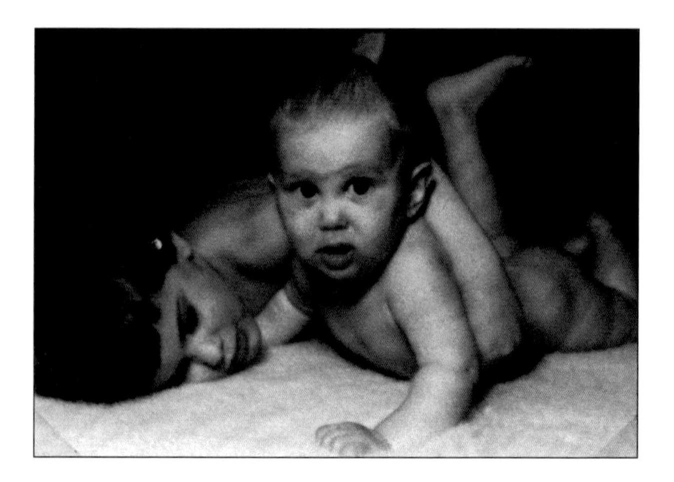

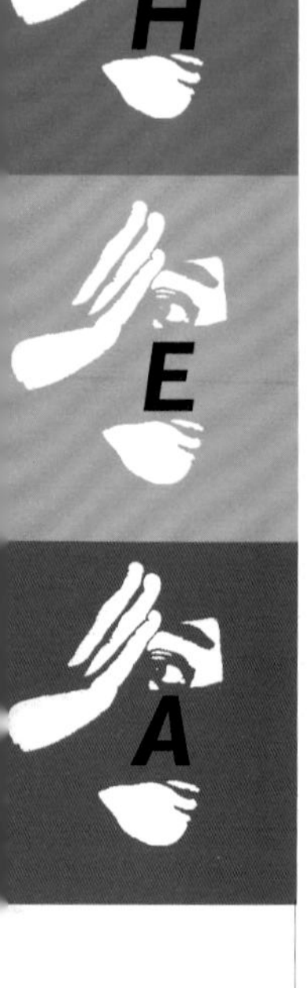

Resources

- Family album photographs or a selection of postcards and found images of a similar style or type
- Scrap-books or albums to collate material in

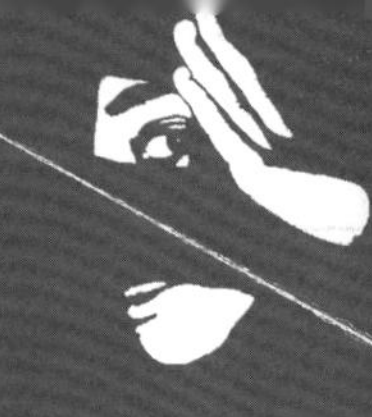

History

'Time-lines'

At George Pringle School, West Sussex, a group of children with moderate learning difficulties worked on a project that developed skills in basic photomontage and mixed media through the production of time-line sequences.[2] Using a combination of images from the family album, found images from magazines and other visual elements, such as maps, the children produced individual pieces that represented their personal life history. Although this project was originally undertaken with Key Stage 3 children, it has been adapted in this context for Key Stage 2. ■

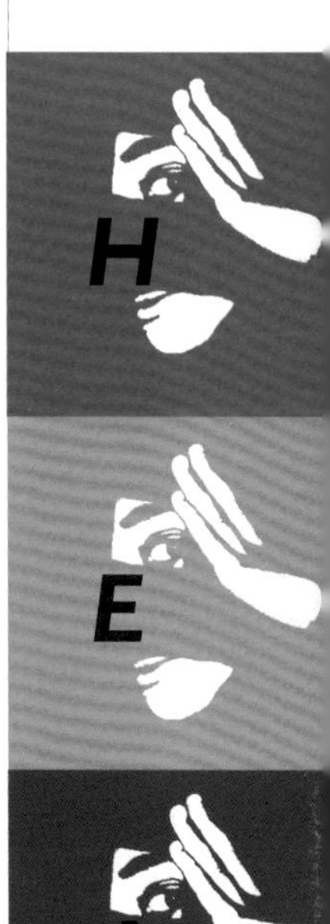

'Time-lines' activities:

- Ask each child to bring in a set of photographs of themselves from babyhood to the present day. These can be photocopied and the originals returned home, and the children can arrange the copies in chronological order to create a time-line.
- Once they have done this ask them to write notes and comments about each photograph or anything of relevance to the time the photograph was taken, for example, their age, friendships, holidays, events, interests, favourite TV programmes and music.
- Children can then go through an editing process which will lead to the typing up of selected captions which can be inserted into their time-lines.
- The final stage is to collect images from magazines, catalogues, maps, etc. to provide more information about their lives. All the elements can be combined to create individual time-lines. ■

Carla Kimber/George Pringle School

Further activity

- Children could create 'future' time-lines by choosing images of people they think they might look like and those who represent the kind of lifestyle they may have when they get older. Again, captions or speech bubbles could be used to anchor meanings. ■

Resources

- Family album photographs
- Photocopier
- Computer/typewriter for captioning
- Range of image resources such as magazines, catalogues and maps

My local history

'People in history from Southwick Green'

At Glebe Middle School, West Sussex, children were asked to focus on an area near to their school called Southwick Green to explore the lives of local historical figures.[3] By using photography as a medium to explore the past these children were given an added enthusiasm for the task of learning about local history. By drawing on a variety of research materials from the school, the local library, interviews with parents and local residents, and old family albums, the project proved that local history can be a rich and rewarding area of study. ■

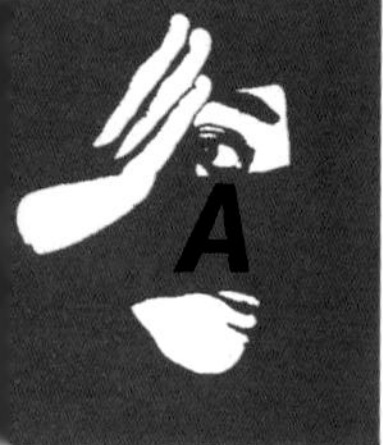

'People in history from Southwick Green' activities

- Having collected resource material about historical figures who lived in your locality work with a group of children to select the characters that they would like to focus on. Once these have been chosen the children can then undertake further research to find out more about their character's occupation and lifestyle and this information can be compiled in sketch or scrap-books.
- Organise a visit to the locality where the chosen characters lived or worked and ask the group to think about the appropriate background for their photographs. These can then be sketched, possibly using a viewfinder, with attention given to framing, angle and distance.

'I'm very proud'

Andrew Weston/Glebe Middle School

Andrew Weston/Glebe Middle School

History

- The next stage is the creation of appropriate costumes for the children to wear. Again the starting point could be sketches. Ideas could be noted down as to the type of pose and expression they might adopt. They could try and depict positive and negative sides of their character and role-play could be used to explore these different character traits.
- Once all the research material has been gathered photographs need to be taken of the selected backgrounds making reference to sketches the children have produced.
- Back at school the children can work in pairs to discuss and plan the portrait photos. As in previous projects if these are taken against a plain background it will be simpler to cut and paste them at the next stage.
- Once the films have been processed portraits can be cut out and montaged on to the landscape backgrounds. The example here is based on Samuel Prosser, Vicar of Southwick in the 17th century, who was so fat he had to be wheeled to church in a barrow, carried and squashed into the pulpit. By photocopying the images first children can play around with scale and there is no risk of photographs being spoiled through accidental cutting.

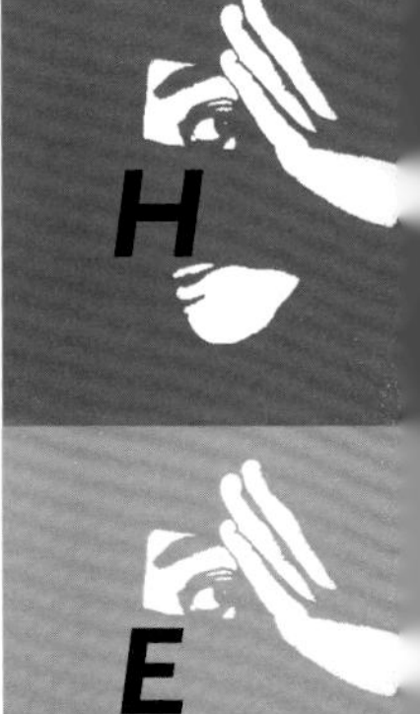

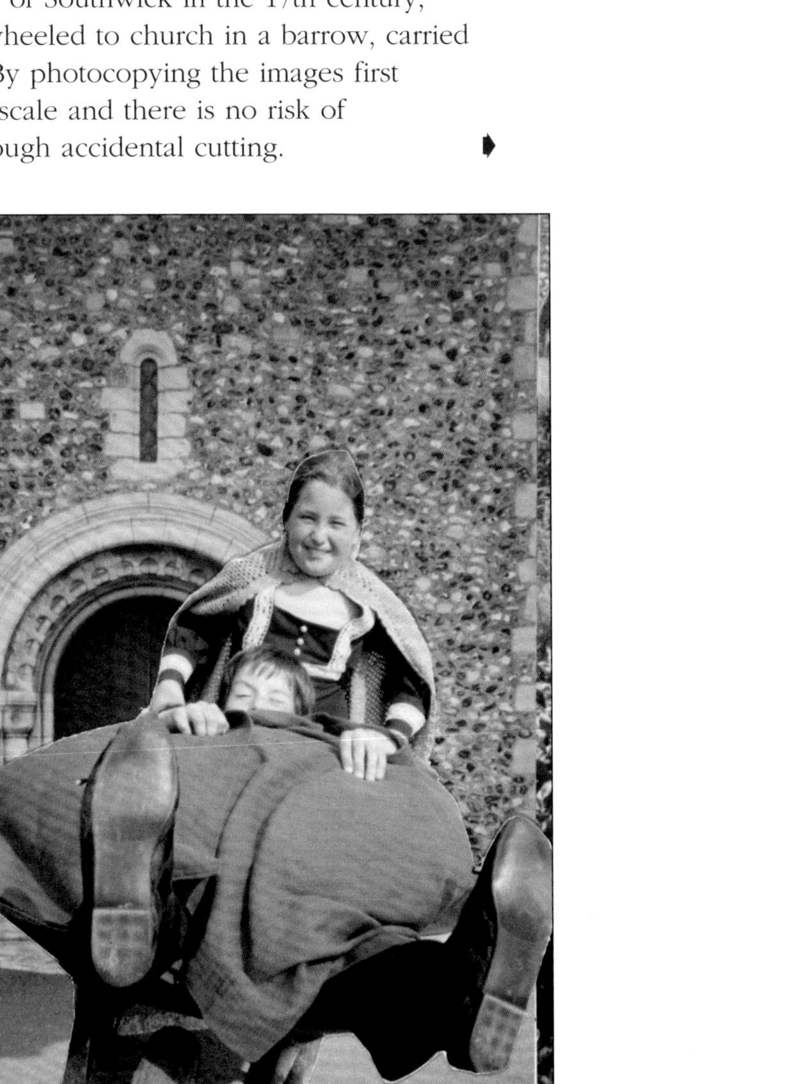

Amie Rice and Michael West/Glebe Middle School

- The finished pieces can be enlarged again on the photocopier and then hand coloured using a range of drawing materials. Children could work on a piece of creative writing placing themselves in the role of their character, which could support their images and the finished work could then be displayed. ■

Andrew Weston/Glebe Middle School

Resources

- Research material on local characters
- Easily accessible local area/environment
- 35mm camera and colour print films
- Paper, pencils, scissors, sketch books, etc.
- Costumes and props

'Roman soldier'

Children and staff at Peel Common Junior School, Gosport, represent one of over forty schools, colleges and institutions throughout Hampshire that participated in the Horizon Project.[4] This was an initiative that gave children and teachers the opportunity to explore the creative development process of multimedia, allowing them to express themselves and their ideas using any appropriate combination of text, photographs, drawings, audio, animation and video. The overall aims of the project were to explore how multimedia could enhance children's learning and to see if it offered teachers a medium through which they could develop resources to support teaching and learning.

Although Hampshire is rich in Roman remains, it proved more cost-effective to hire a living history group to visit the school than to take a party of children by coach to an archaeological site. Three members of Secunda Legion Augustus spent a day 'camped' at the school, impersonating a Roman soldier, nobleman and lady, complete with artefacts, including the soldier's tent and travelling gear. The children worked in groups 'interviewing' the visitors and taking digital photographs with a Canon Ion still video camera. The camera was then linked directly into the computer and the images appeared instantly on the screen. Other children created original graphics using an art package on the computer. All the children were involved in formal research into Roman times providing resources for the final multimedia programme. For further information on computers and digital cameras see the technical tips chapter. ■

History

'Roman soldier' activities

- Arrange for a living history group to visit the school or organise a school visit to introduce the children to aspects of life in Roman times. Using either a traditional 35mm camera or, if available, a digital camera ask the children to document the event or visit, focusing on particular activities, articles of clothing, artefacts, etc.
- Using resources from the school library and the local library ask the children to research and collate information about this period in history, either in their own scrap or note books or in a large class book or folder. This stage of the project could also involve children in creating drawings or graphics on paper, or by working directly on the computer, and writing poems or songs about the Romans.
- Once all the material has been collated the next stage is to input it into the computer. This can be input directly using word processing or graphics packages, or if the work has been generated as paper copy it can be scanned using a colour image scanner.
- Children can then work on the computer using a multimedia authoring package, which in this particular project was the software package *Genesis*, to produce an interactive piece of work containing information and images about different aspects of life in Roman times. For detailed information see *The Horizon Report*, Hampshire Microtechnology Centre. ■

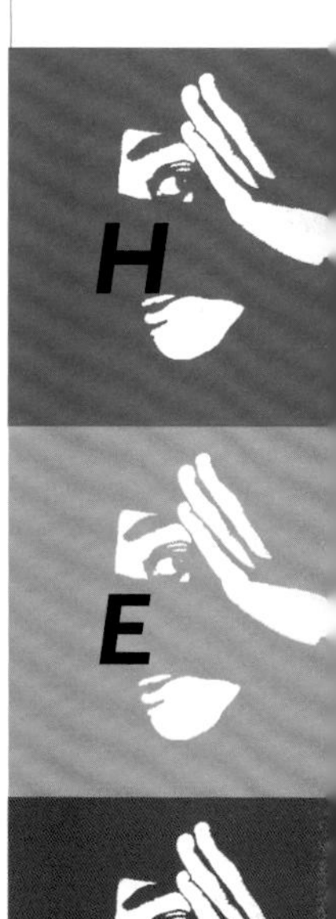

Peel Common Junior School

Resources

- Visit by a living history group or visit to an archaeological site
- Acorn computer and *Genesis* software package or other multimedia computer and authoring package
- Canon Ion camera (may be available for loan from local teachers' centre) or 35mm camera, colour print film and image scanner (access through teachers' centre or local media centre)

People who lived before me

'The Ancient Greeks'

When teaching ancient history an accessible starting point is to make direct comparisons between experiences and activities that take place in everyday life today with those that took place in the past. At Crawley Down Middle School, West Sussex, a class studying the Ancient Greeks were asked to choose an everyday activity to re-enact which was as relevant to the Greeks as it is to people today.[5] By using photography as an exploratory medium this historical period was brought alive for these children.

Part of the project involved discussion about the differences between photographs of original or 'authentic' artefacts, and contemporary book illustrations or film stills from Hollywood costume dramas. The children were fascinated by the differences between the ages and the uses to which the different types of images were put. A key issue was that modern-day pictures showed the work of artists and designers attempting to represent an idea about how life in Ancient Greece may have looked, whereas the original artefacts were mainly made for religious, commemorative and symbolic reasons.

The following activities could be adapted to most periods of history and the results would be just as effective. ■

'The Ancient Greeks' activities

- Using books as research material the children should choose an activity to photograph, for example, eating, cooking or making clay pots, that is relevant to both the past and the present. Once they have decided on an activity they can make preparatory drawings for a present-day photograph.
- Using the resources they have found they should then plan their image of the past focusing on props, costumes, locations and poses. Each child should also choose an image that they can use as a suitable background to montage this photograph on to at a later stage.
- Planning sheets can be used by each child to record their chosen activity in the past and the present, the mood they want to convey, what will be happening in their photographs, the props needed, where the camera will be in terms of angle and distance, and where the light source will come from. To give more meaning to both pose and expression each child could make up a story built around their activity.
- Ask the children, working in pairs, to set up their contemporary photographs in an appropriate area, paying close attention to their planning sheets.

Sarah Gilbert/Crawley Down Middle School

- When taking the images from the past it would be helpful to set up an area with a neutral backdrop as this will make it easier to cut the images out later and will also make it clearer for photocopying. Again, the children should keep referring to their planning sheets.

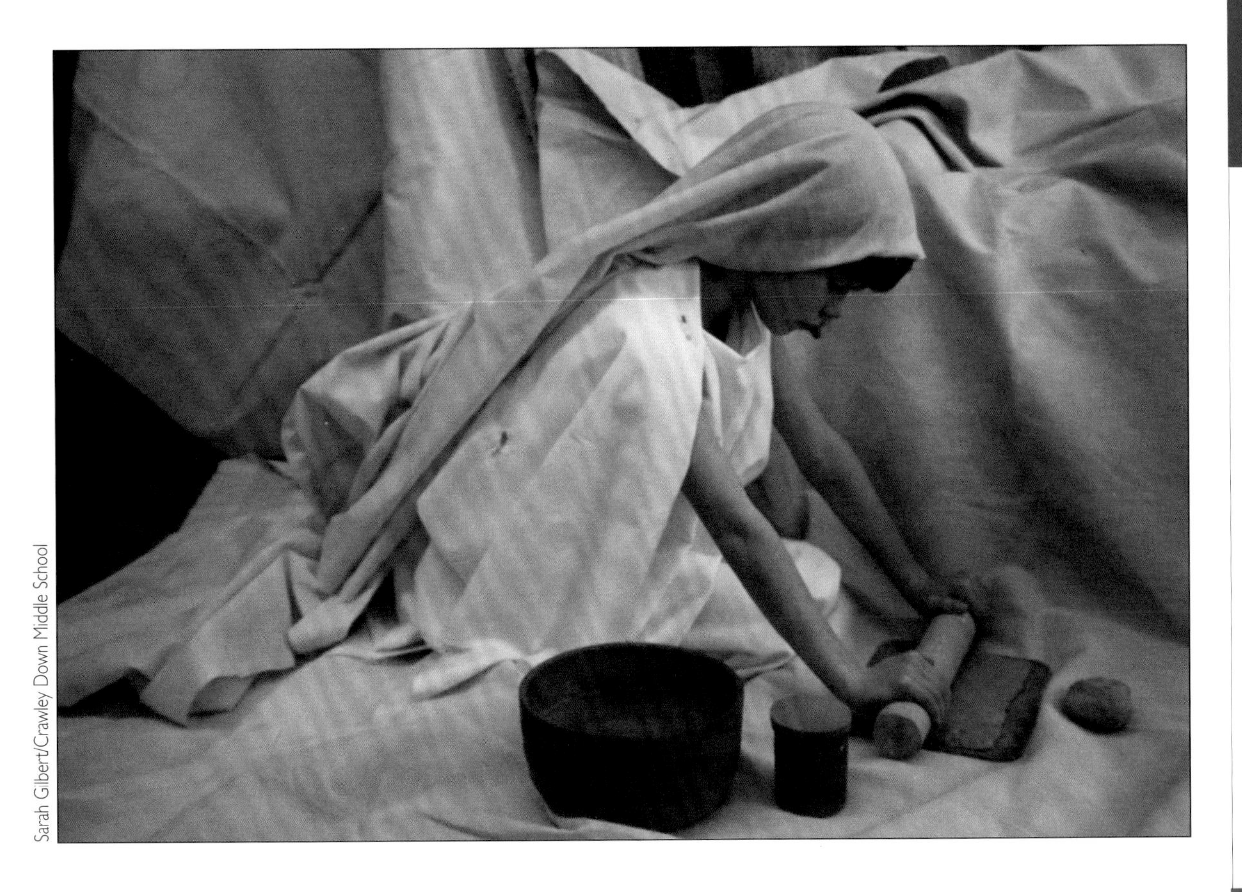

Sarah Gilbert/Crawley Down Middle School

History

- Once the films have been processed the photocopier can be used to enlarge both the children's own photographs and their found images to the correct scale. They can then be montaged together and worked on with colour to integrate the images further. ■

Sarah Gilbert/Crawley Down Middle School

'We thought the pictures wouldn't come out because of not having taken photos before, or because the person taking the picture thought they were no good at photography. Some pictures didn't work because the camera wobbled or because bits got chopped off. But most of the pictures were excellent.'

'Using the worksheets helped some of us, but they were hard to do. They were useful for getting the pictures right.'

'Taking the photos helped us to get ideas for the story, but it was difficult for some people to make the story fit with the pictures. When Rowena took Ben's picture she used the wrong eye to look through the camera, so he got cut in half on the photograph. His photomontage turned out good because he made a weird picture with it. In the story he's a slave hiding behind a tree eating grapes. He's hiding because he doesn't want to be seen.'

The children

Resources

- Research material on the Ancient Greeks
- 35mm compact camera
- Colour print films
- Paper, pencils, scissors, sketch books, etc.
- Costumes and props
- Access to a photocopier

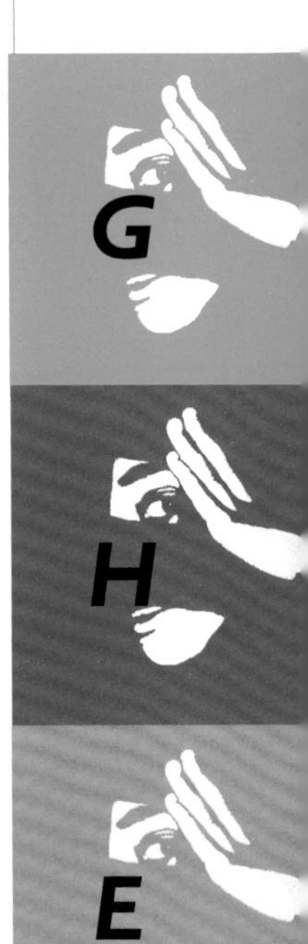

'The Victorians'

At Bigland Green Primary School, London, children embarked on a project about the Victorians that concentrated on a broad theme of 'people, travel and work'.[6] They were encouraged to explore the similarities and differences between the present day and the Victorian era through a combination of their own photographic practice and research into and use of historical material. During the project they came to understand that the lives of the Victorians were affected by changes in industry and transport in much the same way that information technologies are changing our lives today. By making these links between different periods in time the children realised that history is not just about past events which are no longer of relevance, but that issues facing people in the past were often not dissimilar to those facing us all today.

All the children involved with the project at Bigland Green Primary were Bangladeshi and much of the discussion focused on the subject of commuting, both locally and globally, and why it is that people are drawn to certain places or areas to look for work. The children began to realise that there has been a shift in global population in this century and that travel has become far more accessible to people around the world.

This particular project is unusual in that it was one element of a much larger event organised by Camerawork, a photographic gallery in East London, known as 'River crossings'. The event involved selected artists and photographers producing a number of site-specific lens-based installations around the East End of London. A photographer in residence was commissioned to work with a group of children from the school and from the outset they knew that their finished work was to be installed on tube station platforms along the East London line. The work therefore had to be accessible to a wide and varied audience made up of commuters. ■

'The Victorians' activities

- Begin by devising a questionnaire with the children that they can take home for their parents to complete, asking about the type of employment undertaken by various family members, if they have ever lived anywhere else and if so where, and what means of transport they use for daily travel.
- When the questionnaires have been returned to school discuss the differences between types of employment and travel in the present compared with those in the Victorian period.
- The next stage is for the children to identify work that people from their local area are involved in and to decide who will photograph which job. Some children may choose to concentrate on employees within the school, such as the cooks and the schoolkeeper, while others may choose local shopkeepers and others working outside the school.

History

- Once the photographs have been taken each child can map out the position of the school in relation to the place where they have chosen to take their photograph as a means of representing geographical space. For some this may mean the route from the classroom to another part of the school, while for others it will involve representing a larger area. They may choose to incorporate elements of their photographs in the maps or they may prefer to keep them as simple drawings.

Tufaal Ahmed/Bigland Green Primary School

- Using any visual resource material available the children should then find an image of workers during the Victorian era that is compatible with the type of work they have chosen from the present. The found image can then be photocopied and the two can be montaged together. Using photomontage as a medium again introduces the concept of constructed imagery and the children can see their own photographs as a starting point for their image-making as opposed to a finished product.

Shuzahan Begum/Bigland Green Primary School

History

- Once they have explored work in the community the children can then go on to look at forms of travel, again making comparisons with the Victorian period. As well as using archive images they could use drawing to extend beyond the frame and to link different photographs together. The results illustrated show these particular children's ability to understand and interpret perspective and scale in a two-dimensional form. ■

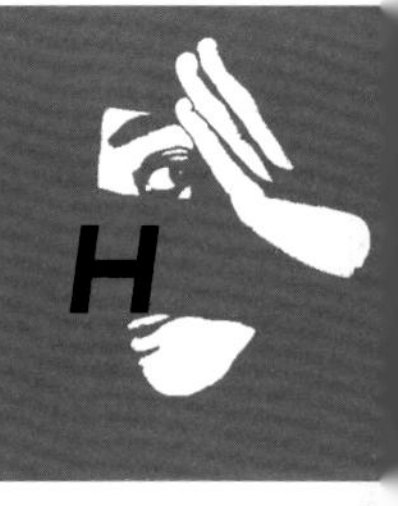

Bigland Green Primary School

Resources

- Visual resource material relating to the Victorian era
- 35mm camera and colour print films
- Paper, colouring pencils, glue stick and scissors

Who makes history?

'Invaders and settlers'

At Holy Cross Intermediate, West Sussex, children enter the school in Year 5 from a variety of Catholic first schools.[7] The two teachers, one with expertise in history and the other in art, chose the topic of 'Invaders' to cover the history study unit 'Invaders and settlers' and decided to approach it in relation to the children's common experience of 'invading' a new school. This was seen as a basis from which the children could express their feelings of insecurity, nervousness and excitement about themselves and their new environment through language and visual images. The teachers felt that this experience would enable these children to empathise with invaders in the past about how they might have felt when leaving home to set out on an expedition somewhere new, while at the same time challenging the stereotype of Vikings and Saxons as marauding barbarians. ■

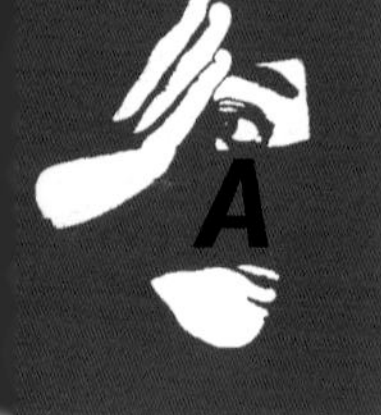

'Invaders and settlers' activities

- Ask the children to write words describing how they feel about being in a new class or school. At the end of the day, or possibly the week, you could repeat the exercise and see if their feelings have changed. If you decide to undertake this project at another point in the year you could ask the children to try and remember how it felt being unfamiliar with their surroundings, with other children or with their teacher, and how they feel now.
- Collect a range of images showing people in situations where they are expressing different emotions and ask the children questions about the content of these images.
- Through a drama activity encourage the class to express different emotions through body movement, making 'freeze-frame' poses of the whole or part of their bodies. Other children could be asked to guess which emotion is being shown.
- Ask the children, working in pairs, to plan two photographs, one of their whole body and one close-up of part of their body. They should consider camera angle, framing, distance and, if possible, lighting. Their plans should be drawn so that their partner can take their photograph as intended.
- From the resulting photographs make enlarged photocopies and ask the children to explore body image, scale and proportion by cutting up the photocopies and reassembling them, creating squashed, stretched or generally altered body images, and then to caption their

resulting images. Through this activity they can be encouraged to explore and express how they feel about themselves and how they think others perceive them. The images could also be worked on with colour in graphic media or collage and text found in newspapers. The children could then consider the relationship between colours and emotions. This part of the project could culminate with a class discussion about the finished pieces, making reference to how the person felt about their image and how others interpreted it.

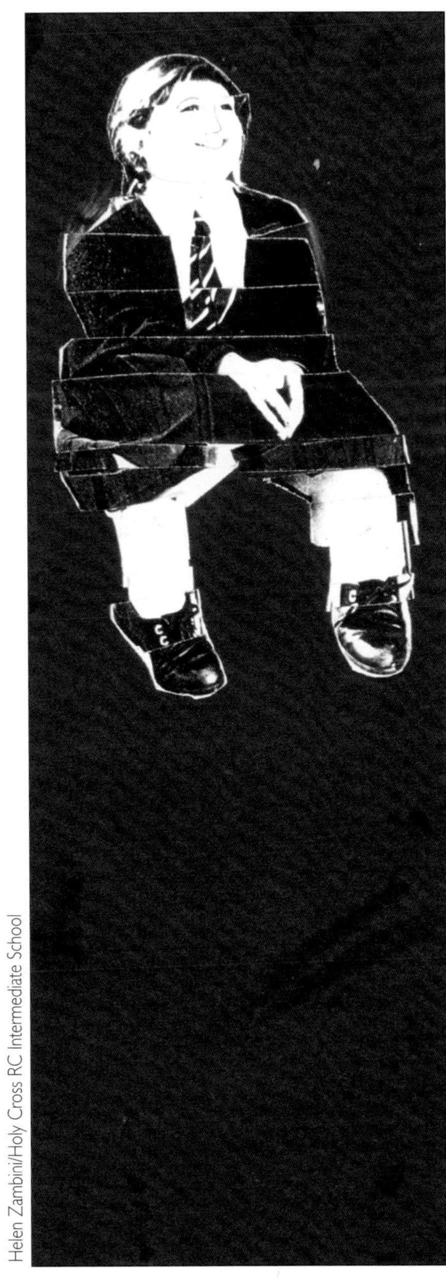

Helen Zambini/Holy Cross RC Intermediate School

- The next stage is to introduce the class to images of invaders. (In this project the teachers used *I Was There*, a book of photographic reconstructions about the Vikings.) Discuss what is happening in the pictures and what the people in them might be feeling. Images could be photocopied and children asked to annotate them.

History

- Provide the class with evidence that shows the invaders from two sides: one representation being the familiar stereotype about fierce marauders, and the other showing a range of artefacts such as pieces from Viking games, decorated jewellery and combs. Raise questions as to whether a savage invader would wear and use such things, or if they might suggest a different kind of person.
- Ask the children to plan and make sketches for a further pair of photographs showing the two opposing views of the invaders. The resulting photographs will then be montaged with backgrounds photocopied from books. They should therefore consider scale and body positions in order to place themselves effectively within their selected background.

Jodie Wells/Holy Cross RC Intermediate School

- Each child's final photomontage could show two aspects of one invader's life, made as a 'reconstruction' of these aspects of life in Viking times. The photocopied backgrounds can be worked on using colour pencils or pastels. ■

Jodie Wells/Holy Cross RC Intermediate School

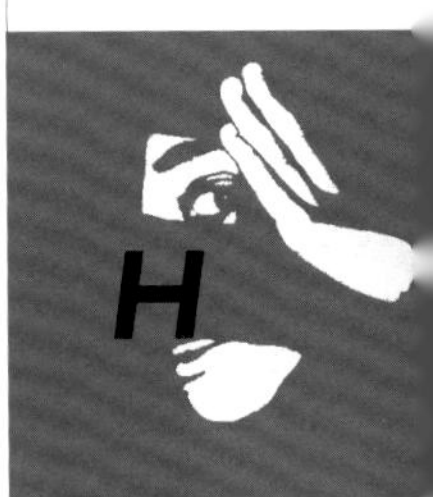

'Pretending to be Vikings and photographing ourselves takes you back to a long time ago. It makes you think about what they did, their art, how they lived, how they dressed, how they might have felt.'

'You don't just learn about different people, we learn in a different way from just reading or asking. Making our own pictures is a different way of learning. It gives you more ideas. I got more interested in mixing things together and getting new ideas.'

'Like in the Viking pictures, it's like you jumped into their world, stepped back in time, and it's because of that that it was fun. It made it easier to learn and you got a lot out of it.'

The children

'For myself, I felt that the class bonded together quickly and any discipline or friendship problems were quickly solved because pupils were aware of how others felt. They developed a critical awareness about the meaning of images and were critical of textbooks showing drawings of stereotypes of invaders. It gave them a sense of purpose to research and seek evidence to support their investigations into the past.'

The teacher

Resources

- Range of images showing people expressing different emotions
- Images of invaders from books such as *I Was There*
- Range of resources on the Vikings
- 35mm camera and colour print films
- Photocopier
- Scissors, glue stick, paper and coloured pencils or pastels

People who changed history

'Heroes and heroines'

As illustrated in other project examples, using images from photographic exhibitions and books as a focus for discussion is often a good starting point for classroom work. *I Dream a World: Black Women Who Changed America* by Brian Lanker, is a collection of portraits and essays that were used with a group of children to introduce the importance of black people's role in history. This photographic history project was organised by Tower Hamlets African Caribbean Association in collaboration with Camerawork, a photographic gallery in East London, and involved an artist in residence working alongside Camerawork's education officer and a class teacher.[8] As part of the project the children were shown a portrait of Rosa Parks. (The book , *Bearing the Cross*, by David J Carrow was used as a reference point.) In Montgomery, Alabama, 1955, when segregation was still in force, she was asked to move to the back of a bus to make room for a white passenger. Her subsequent arrest sparked a 381-day bus boycott, which ignited the civil rights movement. Other figures from history could be studied in the same way depending on the emphasis you want to give the project.

By focusing on an historical event such as this, issues that can affect children's lives in the present can be explored through role-play, and photographic images can be constructed that place the children literally into a visual representation of that event. ■

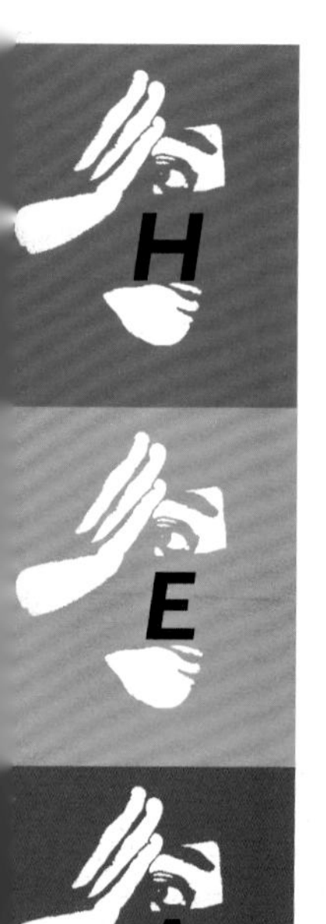

'Heroes and heroines' activities

- Using a large sheet of paper to gather information begin by asking the children where they were born, where their parent(s) were born and where they think their grandparent(s) were born. The intention is to illustrate that we all carry with us ancestry from places that we may know very little about but that will, in some way, have contributed to the way we live and the people we are now.
- Once all the children's contributions have been written down ask them to think about ways in which they could represent their personal history in a single image. They could think about the possible use of symbols, objects, costumes, existing photographs and location or backgrounds as means of illustration. Items could be brought in from home for the photographs.
- Having looked at the children's personal history the next stage is to introduce the children to a chosen historical figure and to discuss any relevant experiences this person may have had. The class can then be encouraged to debate what they might do if they were in this person's shoes. By drawing on the example of Rosa Parks the

children were presented with a scenario in order to raise questions about changes that have taken place over the decades in relation to discrimination and racism.

- Role-play situations can then be constructed around these events as a way of stimulating discussion, and photographs can be used to document the process. In the example given of Rosa Parks a bus was simulated with rows of chairs and each member of the group was given a part to play, with one child experiencing discrimination, and not being allowed to sit down because of the colour of their clothes.

Richard Atkins Primary School

Richard Atkins Primary School

It would obviously be up to individual teachers' sensibility as to the reason for 'exclusion' they might choose in such a scenario. It is important to choose something simple and to be careful not to reinforce prejudices by using hair/eye colour in the role playiing.

- Again, using the scenario of Rosa Parks as an example, ask the children to collect found imagery relevant to the chosen historical event. In this instance it was images of buses, bus tickets, pictures of demonstrations and a portrait of Rosa Parks. Some of these were copied to make slides (see the PSHE and RE chapter, 'I dream of being': Part 2).
- The slides can be projected on to a white wall or screen in a darkened room and the children can step into the images. In the project illustrated, the children attempted to show defiance in their pose and used props such as bus tickets or images of demonstrations which were of direct relevance to the event they were reconstructing. ■

Resources

- Large sheet of paper and marker pen
- Props, costumes, etc. for personal history images
- *I Dream A World* or other historical portraits
- Costumes and/or props for role-play
- 35mm camera and colour print film
- Found images from magazines, newspapers, postcards, etc., some made into slides
- Slide projector
- White sheet

Project credits

1. 'Family albums': Bournhall JMI School, Hertfordshire. Key Stage 2.
   Kim Walden, animateur and Margaret Harris, class teacher
2. 'Time-lines': George Pringle School, West Sussex. Key Stage 3.
   Jenny Fox, advisory teacher and Jan Ridon, class teacher
3. 'People in history from Southwick Green': Glebe Middle School, West Sussex. Key Stage 2.
   Jenny Fox, advisory teacher and Sharon Coombes, class teacher
4. 'Roman soldier': Peel Common Junior School, Hampshire. Key Stage 2.
   'The Horizon Project': Hampshire Microtechnology Centre, Acorn Computers and Jan Field, class teacher
5. 'The Ancient Greeks': Crawley Down Middle School, West Sussex. Key Stage 2.
   Jenny Fox, advisory teacher and Chris Frith, class teacher
6. 'The Victorians': Bigland Green Primary School, London. Key Stage 2.
   Camerawork Gallery, Kamina Walton, photographer and Anyta Parry, class teacher
7. 'Invaders and settlers': Holy Cross RC Intermediate School, West Sussex. Key Stage 2.
   Jenny Fox, advisory teacher and Julia Cook, class teacher
8. 'Heroes and heroines'. Key Stage 2.
   Original idea devised by Tower Hamlets African Caribbean Association, London, Camerawork Gallery and Dave Lewis, photographer in residence. Enacted by children from Richard Atkins Primary School, London ■

History planning grid

Key Stage	Project	Area of study	Key elements
1	Family albums	1ab	1b 4a 5
1	Time-lines	1a	1ab 4a 5
2	Southwick Green	5b	4ab 5abc
2	Roman soldier	1a 2a	2a 4ab 5abc
2	The Ancient Greeks	4a	2a 3a 4ab 5c
2	The Victorians	3a	2c 5c 4ab
2	Invaders and settlers	1c 2c	2abc 4a 5c
2	Heroes and heroines	7c	1a 2abc 4a5c

Science

How do I understand the world?

How do we understand it?

How do I understand the world?

Aims

- To enable children to explore and investigate their surroundings and record their findings using photography.
- To provide a practical and accessible means of exploring and experimenting with physical processes through the workings of light-sensitive materials and cameras.
- To help children in their investigation of the human body and animal and plant life by drawing on photographic evidence of life processes and living things.
- To give children appropriate opportunities to develop and apply an information technology capability to the study of science.

Science seeks to develop an understanding of the world in terms of its living creatures and plants, materials and physical processes. Photographic processes have often been applied in primary education as a means of exploring basic scientific principles at both Key Stages 1 and 2.

The photographic medium enables children to investigate the properties of light and optics actively through the creation of sun pictures, photograms and pinhole cameras. These activities demonstrate the effects of daylight and artificial light on light-sensitive materials, and the ways in which light travels and patterns of light can be recorded. However, because photography is perceived as an essentially practical activity, less attention has been paid to the interpretation of photographs and their application in teaching science. Photographs are often used as a way of bringing the outside world into the classroom, providing visual scientific evidence, but by teaching children to 'read' these photographic representations, as in all other curriculum subjects, the images themselves become open to investigation.

Photography can be used to develop skills in observation, gathering evidence, communicating research findings and experimentation, and so developing children's understanding of scientific processes. Life processes and living things can be documented through photography. The human life cycle can be studied using photographs of the children themselves from birth to the present, and photographs of family members can be used to understand the longer-term effects of aging. Photo-technologies such as X-rays and ultrasound scans provide ways of looking at the composition and structure of the internal workings of the human body. Existing work by photographers such as Eadwærd Muybridge illustrates how humans as well as animals and birds move. Muybridge invented a technique whereby he could record a movement sequence in a series of still images and, by viewing these images in rapid succession through a flick book, create the appearance of movement, thus providing the first important step towards moving pictures.

Close-up photography can provide evidence of animal and plant life and can help in the investigation of their natural habitats. Through photo-montage techniques and computer image manipulation children can take on the identity of other living creatures and place themselves in their environments, thus

stimulating their imagination and providing a clearer understanding of these creatures' habitats.

Existing images from advertising and food packaging can provide a starting point for discussions around issues of health, and children can be encouraged to look critically at the ways in which images are used to manipulate their audience and sell products irrespective of whether they are of any benefit to the consumer.

At Key Stage 2 children are introduced to the solar system. Satellite pictures have enabled us to see the earth from space and these images can be used to prompt questions about the spherical nature of the earth and moon, their orbits and position in relation to one another. ■

How does it work?

The recording of images on to sensitised paper was first discovered in the 1830s by Fox Talbot, a landowner and amateur scientist. By dipping writing paper in silver chloride, leaving it to dry and then placing objects, such as leaves and lace, on to the paper and exposing it to sunlight he could create an image. He then realised that the image could be fixed by using a strong salt solution on the paper after exposure, producing some of the first permanent sun pictures. From Victorian times photography has been seen as both an art and a science and early photographic discoveries were made by both scientists and artists.

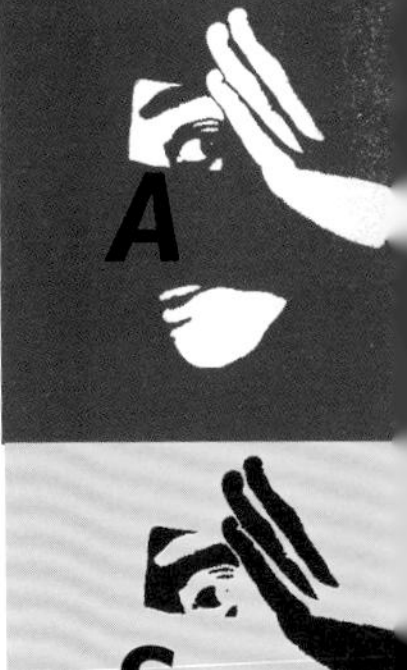

The first three activities in this chapter combine elements of both the science and art curriculum. They give a step-by-step account of ways in which children can learn about the scientific behaviour of light, designing and making images by exposing light-sensitive paper to sun or electric light. The first two of these activities take place in the classroom and require no darkroom or safelighting, while the third requires a darkened room and a red safelight. However, in all three activities the box of photographic paper must be protected from light when taking individual sheets out, either by placing it in a film-changing bag or in a couple of black bin liners.

Whenever using photographic chemicals it is important to go through the safety procedures with children beforehand in order to establish good working practice. Developer and fixer can irritate sensitive skin and stain clothes if not used carefully, therefore tongs or plastic gloves should always be used and aprons should be worn to protect clothing from chemical splashes. Children should always wash their hands after working with chemicals, even when using gloves or tongs. ■

'Sun pictures'

Woodstock School, Bristol, is a special school for primary aged children with emotional and behavioural difficulties.[1] The children come to the school having 'failed' in their mainstream schooling and therefore have negative attitudes to education in general and often have very low self-esteem.

One of the aims of the school is to motivate the children to develop a responsive attitude to learning and working with others while also building up their self-image. Photography has proved a very successful medium through which these aims can be achieved, and through simple processes the children have discovered that they can create sophisticated images. Sun pictures and photograms are seen as an excellent introduction to photographic processes and darkroom procedures, giving the children an opportunity to build up their confidence and skill in handling light-sensitive material before moving on to other more complex approaches. ■

'Sun pictures' activities

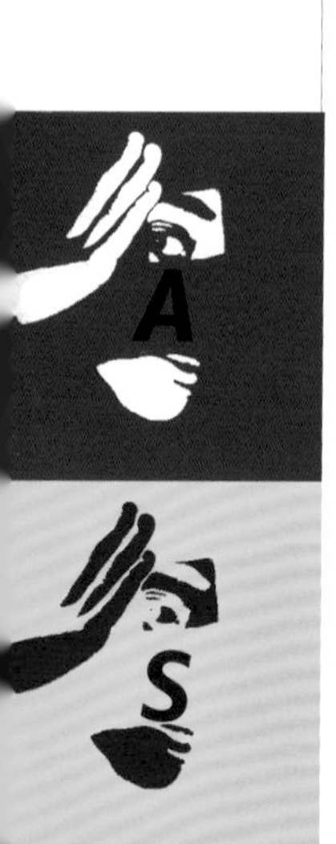

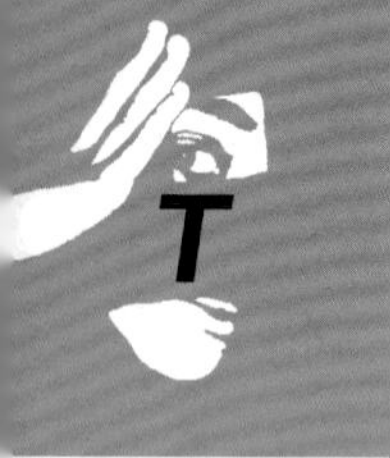

- To create their sun picture each child will need to collect items such as leaves, feathers, grasses, flowers, or any other flat objects that have an interesting shape.
- They can then make rubbings of some of their items using pencils and crayons, or, if using leaves, prints can be made with paint and printing ink. The results will show that leaves with hard and pronounced skeletal lines will produce the clearest images for these rubbings, whereas when the children come to make their sun pictures they will discover that thinner leaves create better images.
- Ask the children to decide how they are going to arrange their items before taking the photographic paper out of the box. This reduces the risk of too much light reaching the paper while they try and decide where to put things.
- To demonstrate the quick reaction of sunlight on photographic paper place the box of paper inside a black bag or bin liner to protect the rest of the box from exposure. Take one sheet of paper out of the box, leaving the rest inside the bag, and holding it in direct sunlight ask the children to observe the rapid change in colour.
- Give each child a piece of hardboard and glass, for example 5x7 inch clip frames. Then, with the box of paper still in a black bag, give a sheet of photographic paper to each of the children and ask them to place it on the hardboard, put their objects on the paper in the position they have chosen and place the glass over the top. This needs to done as quickly as possible and the layers should then be secured using clips to ensure good contact and to keep things in place.

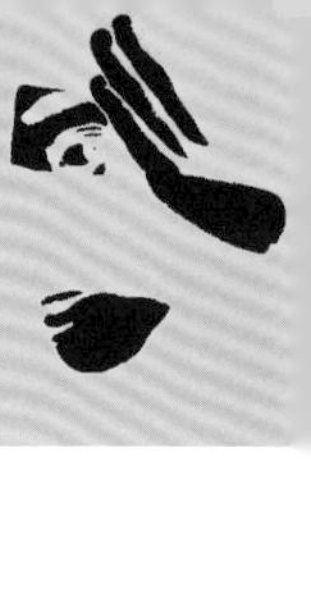

Woodstock School

- They should then move the frame as quickly as possible into the sunlight. The amount of time to leave the paper in the sunlight will depend on the strength of the light and will require experimentation. It may take less than a minute or as long as 30 minutes to produce good results, depending on the strength of the sun. The children could also experiment by exposing paper at different times of the day.
- As soon as the paper has turned a dark colour it should be taken out of the frame quickly and put into a tray of fixer for the recommended time. The paper should then be washed under running water for at least five minutes and then dried. The images will change colour in the fixer and again when they dry.
- Despite fixing, sun pictures will fade over a number of weeks whether kept in bright or subdued light. One way of producing a permanent image is to photocopy it soon after it has dried. However, the number of copies you can make is limited as the light from the photocopier will also cause the image to fade. ■

Resources

- Leaves, feathers, grasses, flowers, etc.
- Crayons, inks, paint for rubbings and prints
- Small piece of hardboard and glass, for example, 5x7 inch clip frames – glass edges should be sanded or covered with masking or gaffer tape to make them safer to handle. Alternatively, acetate sheets and bulldog clips or clear perspex could be used.
- Bulldog clips or similar
- Photographic paper
- Black bag, bin liner or film-changing bag to put the paper box in when removing sheets
- Fixer and tray (or plastic drawer)
- Tongs or plastic gloves

Science

'Cyanotypes'

Chelsea and Westminster Children's Hospital School embarked on a series of collaborative photography workshops with The Photographers' Gallery, London, entitled 'Myself and my environment'.[2] Over the course of the workshops children were introduced to a range of photographic techniques through which they were encouraged to explore aspects of their physical identity, these included photograms, chemograms, photo-batik and cyanotypes.

The cyanotype process was traditionally used to produce prints known as architect's blueprints. It involves coating cartridge paper with a mixture of iron salts to create a photo-emulsion which produces deep blue prints when the paper is exposed to light and then developed. At the hospital the children's own X-rays were used to create images through the cyanotype process, working on the same principle as sun pictures. The iron salts used are available from chemical suppliers, or, alternatively, the chemistry departments of secondary schools or colleges. Although care should be taken when using them, the working solutions contain only very small quantities of chemicals and are therefore quite safe to use with young children. However, as when working with other chemical solutions, children should wash their hands afterwards. ■

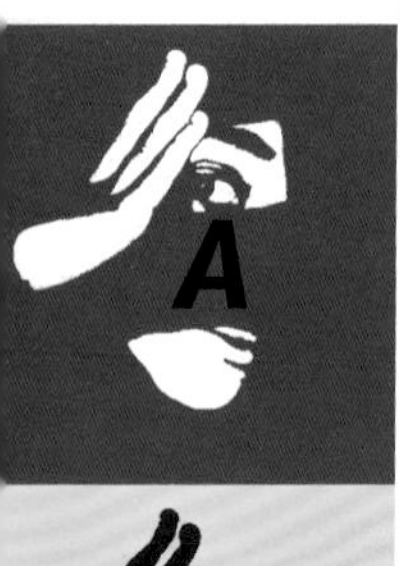

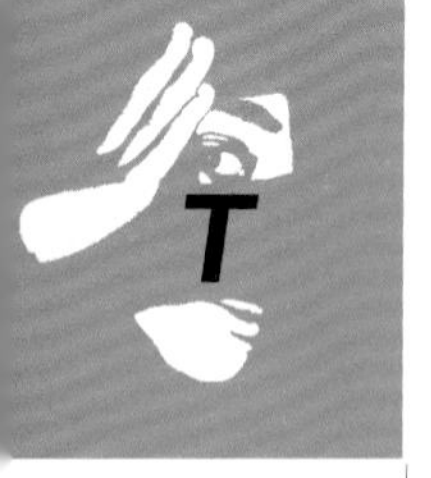

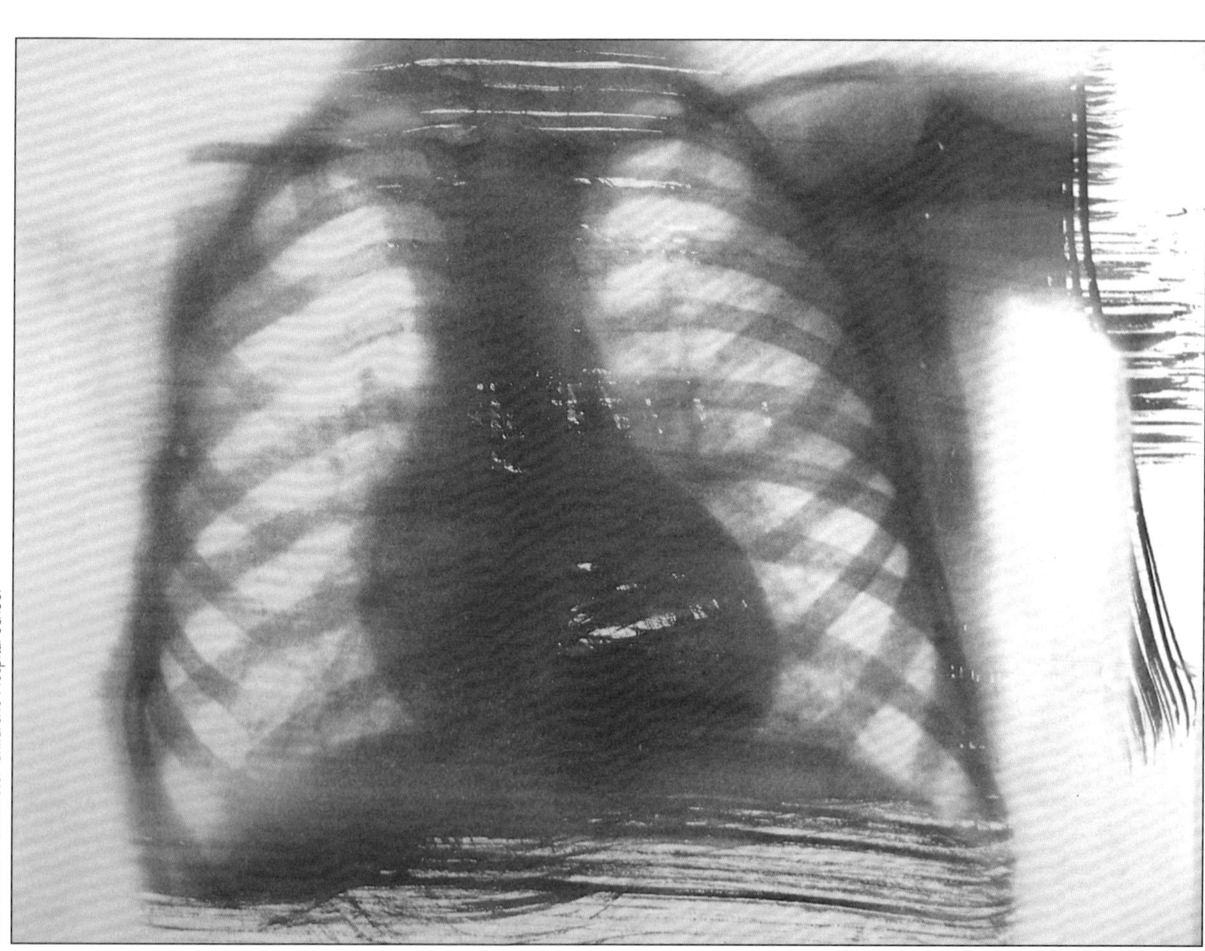

Chelsea and Westminster Children's Hospital School

'Cyanotypes' activities

- Mix the 20g ferric ammonium citrate with 100ml of water. Then mix the 8g potassium ferricyanide with 100ml of water. The two solutions should be combined.
- Ask the children, working in dim room light away from direct sunlight, to brush the surface of white cartridge paper evenly with a thin coat of the solution, then dry it quickly with a hairdryer. As long as it is kept in the dark this sensitised paper will now keep for up to a week.
- The children then need to select items to place on the sensitised paper to make their cyanotype images. At the hospital, some children used their own X-rays, but personal possessions and other objects could be used. Alternatively, they could produce acetate photocopies of parts of their bodies, or photocopy existing photographs of themselves on to acetate. Acetate will produce similar results to those achieved with an X-ray as it acts as a giant negative, creating a positive cyanotype image on the paper.
- As with the sun pictures the children should place their acetates, etc. on to the sensitised paper away from sunlight and secure with a clip and a sheet of glass or clear plastic.
- The clipped acetates should then be moved into direct sunlight. The exposure times for cyanotypes tend to be longer than those for sun pictures and in bright sunshine exposure may take up to five minutes. Again, the children will need to experiment to find the correct time needed.
- When the paper turns a yellowish-brown colour it should be developed in running water for five minutes. During this time the image will become darker, the contrast will become more defined and the image will turn a strong blue colour .
- The prints should then be left to dry. ■

Resources

- White paper
- 20g ferric ammonium citrate (green crystals or powder will work faster than the brown) plus 100ml water
- 8g potassium ferricyanide plus 100ml water
- Paint brushes

'Photograms'

At Woodstock School, Bristol, a pottery cupboard is converted into a darkroom each time photography activities take place.[3] There is a well-organised system for darkroom-based work at the school whereby children work in pairs, one child concentrating on creating an image while the other takes responsibility for all the timing involved. This system works very effectively as children have to depend on each other, encouraging responsibility and trust between them. Other benefits are their increased ability to listen and follow instructions, manual dexterity, the understanding of chemical processes and language, and a respect for safety and good working practices.

When creating photograms it is necessary to have access to a darkened room, but if using a room with windows black sugar paper or bin liners can be used to block out the light. You will need to set up the chemical trays in advance and, unlike sun pictures, to make a photogram you will need developer as well as water and fixer. It is useful if there is a water source in the room itself, or nearby, to wash the finished prints. ■

'Photograms' activities

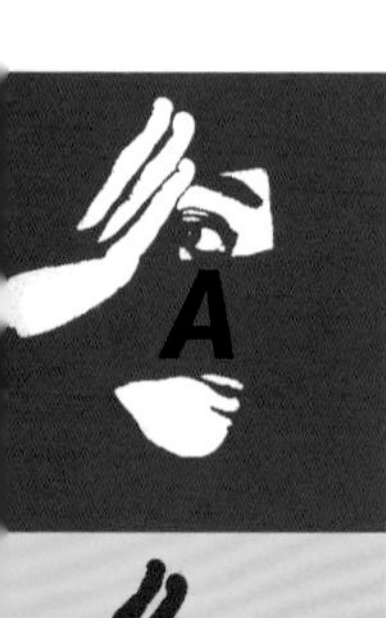

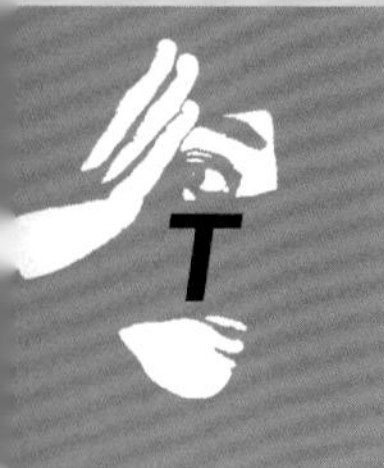

- Collect together a range of objects, both natural and synthetic, that the children can use to make their photograms, such as toothbrushes, small toys, fishbones, fabrics, netting, plants, etc.
- Ask the children to design a picture by selecting objects and placing them on a ordinary piece of paper. They could be drawn around to remind the children of their positioning.
- Working in a darkened room with a red safelight, torch or lamp covered with red gel, take out a sheet of photographic paper and ask the children to position their objects in the same way on this paper.
- Once they are in place the children will need to expose the paper to white light. The more focused the light source the sharper the results will be. As with the sun pictures you may need to experiment to calculate the best exposure time and the distance between the light source and the paper, but it is unlikely to be more than a few seconds.
- The children should then place the paper in the developer tray, making sure it is completely covered, and process for the recommended time, gently agitating the tray throughout.
- The paper is then transferred into a second tray filled with water and agitated for 30 seconds to stop development, and then moved into the fixer tray for the recommended time.
- The prints must then be washed in running water for at least five minutes and dried.
- Once they are dry a reversal image can be produced from the original print by contact printing, that is, instead of white objects on

Ross Black/Woodstock School

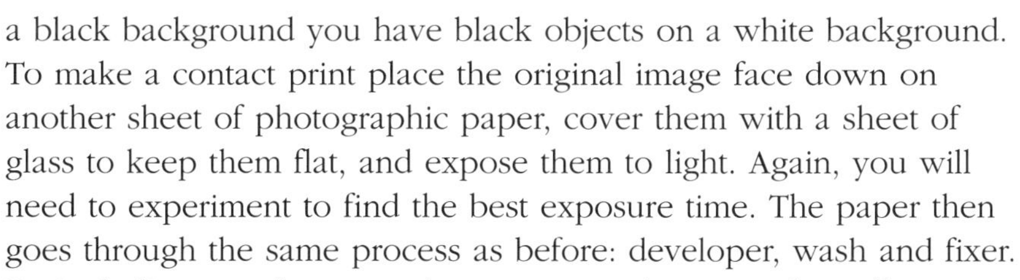

a black background you have black objects on a white background. To make a contact print place the original image face down on another sheet of photographic paper, cover them with a sheet of glass to keep them flat, and expose them to light. Again, you will need to experiment to find the best exposure time. The paper then goes through the same process as before: developer, wash and fixer.

- By including translucent and transparent objects in the collection there is the opportunity to study some more advanced properties of light and how light behaves when it can pass through objects and affect the photographic paper. ■

Ross Black/Woodstock School

Resources

- Darkened room
- Black sugar paper or bin bags to cover windows if necessary
- Range of opaque, translucent and transparent objects
- Photographic paper
- Developer, fixer, water and three trays
- Tongs or plastic gloves
- Desk lamp or torch as source of white light
- Red safelight, torch or lamp covered with a red gel

'Pinhole cameras'

The construction of pinhole cameras is a popular introduction to photography in primary education, allowing the recording of a negative image on to photographic paper or film. The basic concept is a black box with a small pinhole at one end that allows light to pass through, thus creating an image at the opposite end – in effect, a simplified version of the way in which light passes through a camera's lens on to the film's surface, or through the human eye on to the retina to form an image. Pinhole photography is an ideal way for children to actively investigate the workings of a camera and to understand the way in which a photographic negative is produced.

At Cavendish First School, Northumberland, a class of 36 children spent a single half-day session working with an advisory teacher.[4] In this time each child managed to produce their own pinhole image. A small cupboard was used as a darkroom and, in order to standardise exposure times, cameras were made up in advance from cans of the same diameter and height. The class was divided into three groups. One group began by making test exposures and once their exposure times had been calculated these were used by the other two groups to make their images. Pinhole cameras can be square, cylindrical or rectangular. Catering-size coffee tins and shoe boxes make good pinhole cameras, but whatever kind of container you choose it must have a tight-fitting lid and be made of material thick enough to prevent light passing through. ■

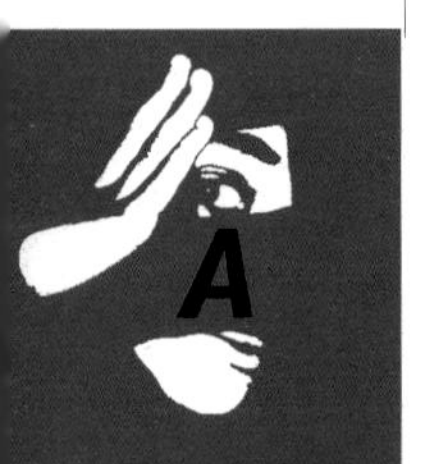

'Pinhole cameras' activities

- Begin by asking the children to paint or cover the inside of their container, including the lid, with matt black paint or paper.
- They should then cut a hole approximately 2cm square in the side of the container. If you are using tins or are working with very young children you may need to do this for them.
- Cut a piece of foil or metal to approximately 4cm square to cover the hole made in the container. Again you may decide to undertake this part of the process yourself.
- Make a hole in the material using a fine needle or sharp compass point. The size and shape of this hole will effect the image created – if it is too large the image will not be pin-sharp, but if it is too small you will need a longer exposure time. However, a smaller hole will usually provide better overall results.
- Ask the children to stick the material firmly over the inside of the hole they have cut in the container, using black tape to fix it in place. Once positioned they should stick a piece of black tape over the pinhole on the outside of the container to act as a lens cap. The container is now a 'camera'.
- In a darkened room, or using a film-changing bag or bin liners,

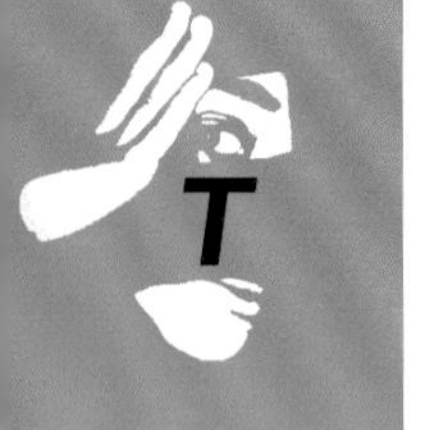

remove the lid of the container and place a piece of photographic paper inside the camera directly opposite the pinhole, making sure the shiny side of the paper faces the pinhole. Keep it in place with Blu-Tack or double-sided tape and then replace the lid.

- The camera is now ready to use. The better the weather conditions are the better the photographs are likely to be. Alternatively, you could use bright spot lights. Exposure times will vary depending on the light available, the size of the pinhole, the distance between the pinhole and the photographic paper, and the type of photographic paper used, therefore a certain amount of trial and error is involved. The camera should be placed on a flat surface and, to ensure it does not move, books or similar heavy objects should be used to weigh it down.
- When they are ready to make their exposure the children should remove the tape from the pinhole. To begin with they should use stationary objects as the subjects for their images. When they are more confident they can experiment by photographing other children but the 'sitters' must remember that they may have to stay perfectly still for a considerable amount of time to prevent the image being blurred. Exposure times may vary from 30 seconds in very bright conditions to six minutes in very dull conditions.
- The pinhole must then be re-covered and the paper taken out in a darkroom under a red safelight.
- The children should process the paper in the same way as ordinary photographic prints – developer, rinse, fixer and wash – but the image that appears will be in negative. To get a positive image the children must make a contact print as described at the end of the photogram activities page. If the results are not satisfactory, for the negative or the positive image, alter the exposure time accordingly, that is, if the image is too dark reduce the exposure time and if it is too light increase the exposure time. ■

Rosie Thornton, Ian Olgivie, Leanne Towart, Stuart Tapson/Cavendish First School

Resources

- An empty tin or box
- Matt black paint or black paper
- Scissors
- Blu-Tack
- Black tape
- Tin foil or thin metal sheet
- Fine needle or compass
- Photographic paper
- Developer, fixer, water and three trays

How do I grow?

As part of their scientific study children will be investigating the human body. Their own photographs can be used to illustrate growth and physical change by charting development from birth to school age, and those of family members can show how the process extends into adulthood and old age. They may also highlight physical similarities from one generation to the next, helping children understand genetic inheritance. The same photographs can generate discussion about climatic change, illustrating how we alter our clothing depending on the weather conditions.

By studying a range of portraiture children are not only seeing examples of human development but also the development of photography itself. When cameras were first invented shutter speeds were very slow and subjects would have to sit perfectly still for long periods of time often with a clamp behind their neck in order to record their image successfully on film. Today, because of increasing shutter and film speeds, we have the ability to 'freeze' a high-speed vehicle in a photograph, and due to technological developments it is even possible to photograph a foetus in the womb or produce an X-ray to explore the internal workings of the body. ■

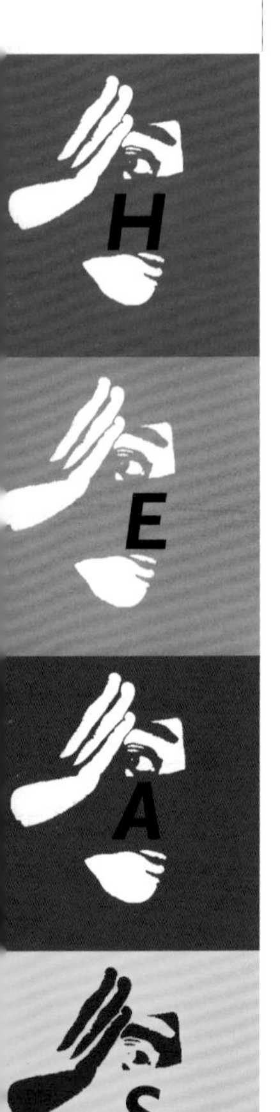

'Growing'

At Southgate First School, West Sussex, a class worked on a project that used existing portrait photographs to explore the early stages of the human life cycle.[5] This project formed part of a larger topic on 'Movement' which is detailed in the art chapter. The children brought in photographs from home that charted their development from birth to the present day and these were photocopied and arranged in chronological order to create a time-line sequence. Notes and comments were then added providing information about their age in each photograph, and in some cases children included photocopies of their birth certificates and hospital tags. ■

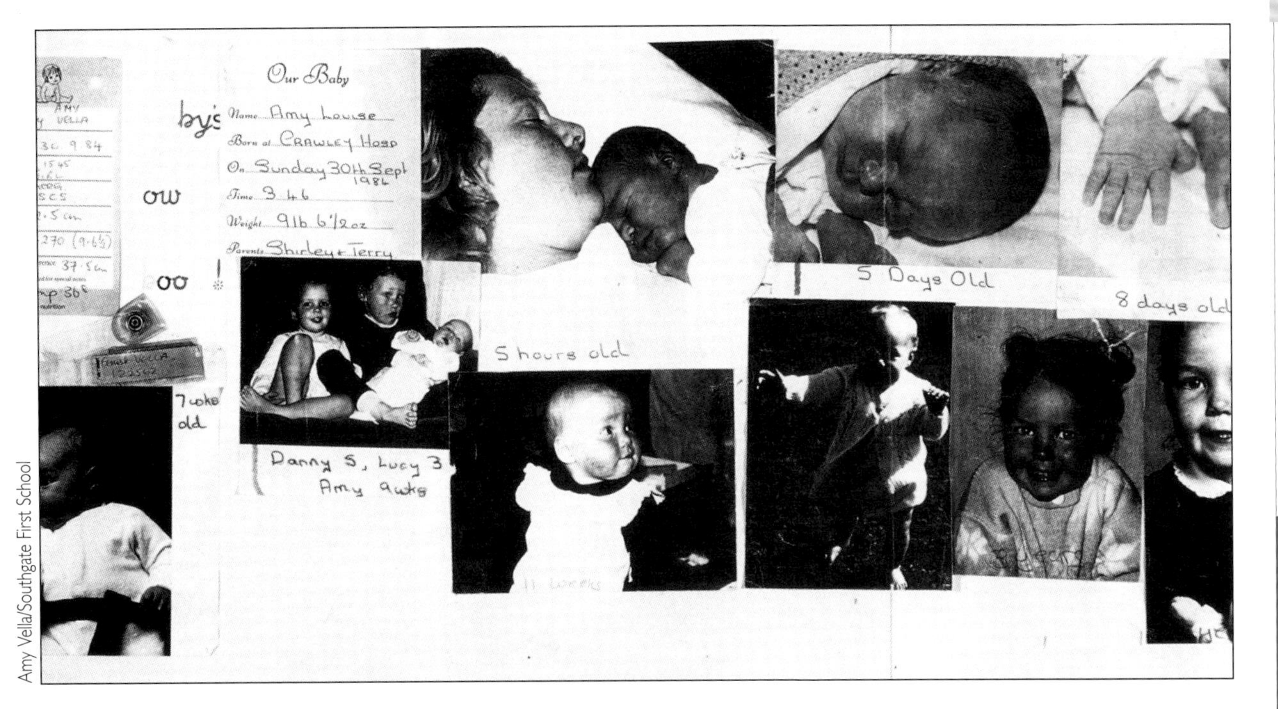

Amy Vella/Southgate First School

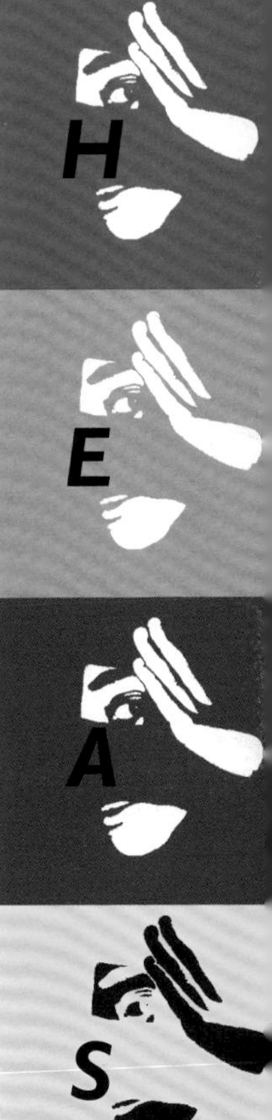

'Growing' activities

- Each child will need to bring in a set of photographs of themselves from babyhood to the present day. If possible this could include an ultrasound scan to illustrate foetal development. A letter should be sent home to parents/guardians explaining the project the children are involved in and making it clear that all photographs will be photocopied and the originals returned.
- The children can then arrange their images in chronological order to create a time-line and write notes and comments that chart their growth and development.
- As an extension of the project, photographs of other family members such as a parent or grandparent could be used. If photographs are available that showed all the stages of a grandparent's life, from babyhood to old age, an extended time-line could be created and further stages of the human life cycle studied. It would also provide an opportunity to look at the changes and development in photographic techniques and approaches to photographic portraiture. ■

Further actvities

- The children could find images of people, houses, cars and places, for example, to construct an imaginary future life. This 'life' would explore how the children might look and what their profession might be. ■

Resources

- Family album photographs
- Photocopier

How healthy am I?

Advertising images for food and drink can be used to initiate scientific study with children about health and nutrition. The visual style and use of text advertising products such as ready meals or alcohol can also be examined in terms of the ways in which advertisers can influence our spending choices, regardless of existing scientific evidence that might show the limited nutritional value or even harmful effects of such products. Children can then produce their own photographs in order to explore all aspects of health education, from diet through to exercise and health in general. ■

'Food – fit for life'

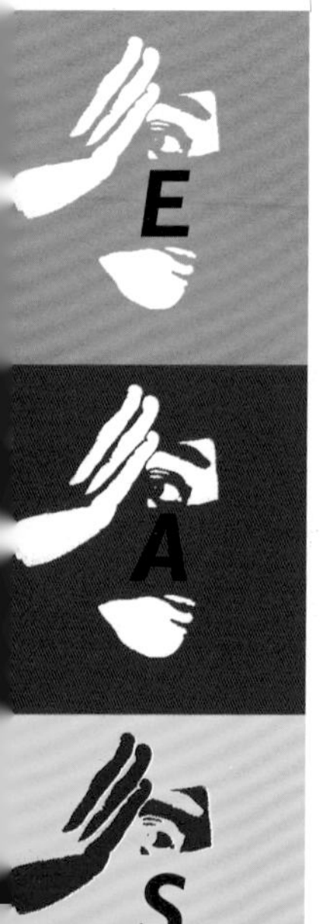

At Broadfield North Middle School, West Sussex, photography was used to explore feelings and attitudes towards food.[6] The class collected a variety of images related to food and eating, including advertisements and food packaging, and spent time decoding them in terms of the language, imagery, typefaces and colour used, and who they thought the consumers might be. The children gradually began to realise that the producers' main concern is selling and they are often manipulative in the ways they go about marketing their products, offering the consumer products to supposedly improve their lives irrespective of whether they are healthy or beneficial in any way.

The children went on to create their own food-related images that were intended to tell a story. These ranged from serious documentary-style scenarios, such as someone undergoing hospital treatment due to poor eating habits, to exaggerated pieces where children surrounded themselves with junk food, making references to unhealthy eating. ■

'Food – fit for life' activities

- Ask the children to bring in a variety of food packaging from home and collect together examples of food advertisements.
- Working as a class, discuss the images used on the packaging and in the adverts, and what effect the language and graphics used have on the potential consumer. At this stage you could ask the children to collect a range of scientific data about personal health, for example the importance of vitamin content in food.
- The next stage is for the children to produce their own images, focusing on some aspect of food-related health. At Broadfield North, the children used collage to combine their own photographs with found images to imply a narrative. However, if the children choose to concentrate on generating their own images they may need props and different types of food to get the results they need.
- As part of the presentation they could create borders for their photographs from food packaging and adverts. ■

Steven Cousins/Broadfield North Middle School

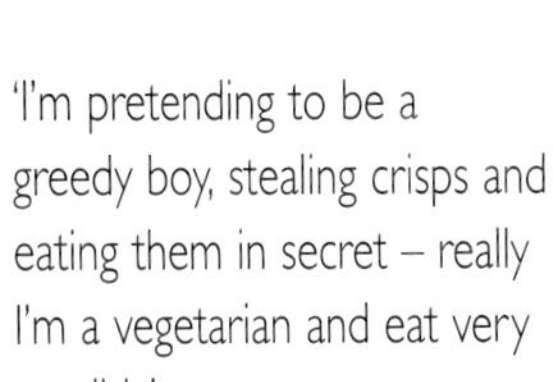
'I'm pretending to be a greedy boy, stealing crisps and eating them in secret – really I'm a vegetarian and eat very sensibly.'

Resources

- Food packaging and adverts
- 35mm camera and colour print film

How do creatures around me live?

Whether through photographs of creatures in their natural habitats or imaginative images that position children in these creatures' place, photography is an ideal medium through which to identify and classify living things. The study of minibeasts is popular in primary education and many books exist of the subject. These creatures, such as wooklice and spiders, are commonly found in homes and gardens in the UK, making them familiar to children and easy to study in their natural habitats. ■

'Minibeasts'

At The Park Primary School, Bristol, a group of children worked with a photographer in residence and the Watershed Media Centre to explore the ways in which new technology can have an impact on the primary curriculum.[7] Taking their science topic on 'Minibeasts' (living things in their environment) as the focus, and drawing on their understanding of metamorphosis, each child chose the identity of a minibeast they wanted to become. The children then imagined themselves as those minibeasts, seeing the world from their point of view and familiarising themselves with their appropriate habitats.

Starting with traditional cut-and-paste techniques and progressing to the use of Apple Macintosh software, *Adobe Photoshop*, the children designed finished images depicting themselves as their chosen minibeast. The computer allowed them to re-scale images in order to paste them together seamlessly, add paint and colour effects and duplicate elements, where necessary, to create highly effective results Similar work could be produced without the use of computers but to produce images of compatible scale would involve time on the photocopier reducing and enlarging elements in order to make them work together as a whole. For further information on computers see the technical tips chapter. ■

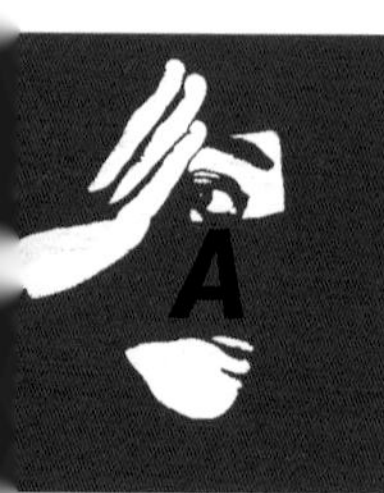

'Minibeasts' activities

- Ask the children, working individually or in pairs, to choose a minibeast that they would like to research in detail, whose identity they would like to take on.

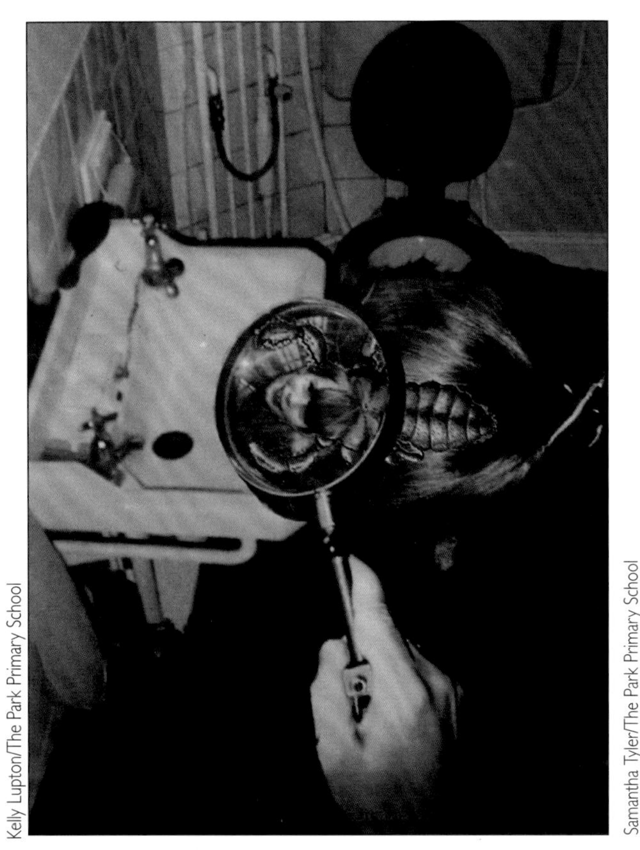
Kelly Lupton/The Park Primary School

Samantha Tyler/The Park Primary School

- Once they have made their choice they will need to look for images of their chosen minibeasts and of the environments in which they live. If these come from books they will need to be photocopied and if working with a computer they should also be scanned and saved.
- The children should begin to compile scrapbooks that contain written ideas, photographs and photocopies of both minibeasts and environments.
- Once they have a clear idea of how they want their finished image to look they should draw it or make a rough cut-and-paste interpretation with a combination of drawing and photocopies.
- They can then begin to plan the photographs they will need to take of themselves, of faces or body parts. They should take into consideration the angle they the photographs will need to be taken from depending on the view of the minibeast.
- When taking their portrait photographs the children should work in pairs; the child being photographed should show their partner their drawing or montage and direct them as to how they want their photographs taken, with regard to facial expression, body position, point of view, etc.
- Once all the elements needed to complete their images have been collected together they can then be photocopied to scale or scanned on to the computer. Although at The Park School an Apple Macintosh computer with *Photoshop* software was used, the work could be produced on any other computer that has a facility to scan and manipulate images. The children can then use the software to alter individual elements in terms of scale or colour, etc. and to bring those elements together to make a finished image. ■

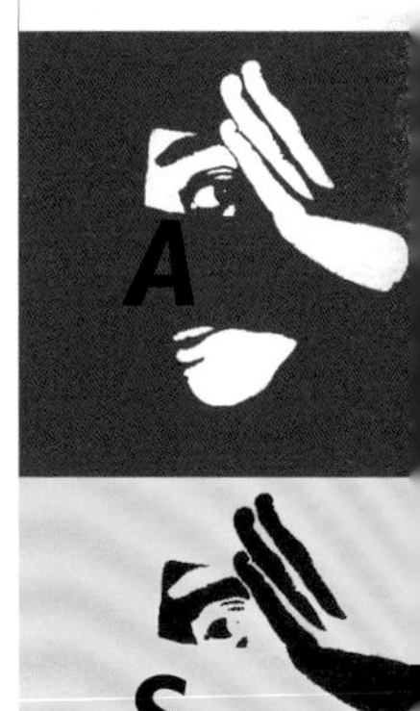

Resources

- Images of minibeasts and their habitats
- Access to a photocopier
- 35mm camera and colour print film
- Computer and image manipulation software
- Image scanner

Project credits

1. 'Sun pictures': Woodstock School, Bristol. Key Stages 1 and 2.
   Lily Lam, support teacher
2. 'Cyanotypes': Chelsea and Westminster Children's Hospital School, London.
   The Photographers' Gallery, London, Joy Gregory, photographer and Rod Hutchinson, teacher
3. 'Photograms': Woodstock School, Bristol. Key Stages 1 and 2.
   Lily Lam, support teacher
4. 'Pinhole cameras': Cavendish First School, Northumberland. Key Stages 1 and 2.
   Chris Madge, advisory teacher, Mrs Dower, class teacher and Miss Machin, classroom assistant
5. 'Growing': Southgate First School School, West Sussex. Key Stage 2.
   Jenny Fox, advisory teacher and Yvonne Davis, class teacher
6. 'Food – fit for life': Broadfield North Middle School, West Sussex. Key Stage 2.
   Jenny Fox, advisory teacher and Lorna Barton, class teacher
7. 'Minibeasts': The Park Primary School, Bristol. Key Stage 2.
   Watershed Media Centre, Kamina Walton, photographer and Chrissy Stiff, class teacher ■

Science planning grid

Key Stage	Project	AT1	AT2	AT3	AT4
1	Sun pictures	1ab 2abc 3acd			3ab
1	Cyanotypes	1ab 2abc 3abd			3ab
1	Photograms	1ab 2abc 3acdf			3ab
1	Pin-hole cameras	1abcde 2abc 3cd			3ab
2	Growing			2g	
2	Food – fit for life			2b	
2	Minibeasts			5ab	

How do I tell it?

English

How do we tell it?

How do I tell it?

At its simplest level the English curriculum is concerned with communication. The subject seeks to develop children's abilities to communicate effectively by looking at questions of language, meaning and interpretation.

When children start school they may not be able to read words but they do possess the ability to 'read' images; in other words, they are, to a degree, visually literate. Photographs can provide a stimulus for talking and writing. Building on their knowledge of reading pictures children can talk more readily about photographs, describing in detail what they see, developing ideas, and listening to similarities and differences of interpretation by different members of the class. In this way images can be used very successfully as a starting point for language work, particularly for children with English as a second language.

Photography has been used successfully within English for some time as a means of understanding the mechanics of story-telling. Narrative structures can be analysed by studying components such as audience, point of view, setting the scene and sequencing, thus providing children with a framework from which to create their own stories. By creating their own photographs and using them in the production of their own narratives children can begin to explore the relationship between pictures and words. Recent developments in new technology and the increasing access to computers in both primary and secondary schools have also opened up new creative possibilities for children's reading and writing through the production of digital narratives.

Existing media images can be used to stimulate discussion in the classroom, highlighting the fictional and factual use of photographs, and to raise questions around issues of representation. Children can learn to deconstruct these images in order to understand how meaning is controlled, and this will enable them to take greater control over the construction of meaning in their own images.

Photography within English can provide a stimulating context in which to deliver the attainment targets: speaking, listening, reading and writing, and also provides an accessible introduction to the process of practical production. ■

Aims

- To develop children's abilities to communicate effectively by looking at questions of language, meaning and interpretation.
- To use photography as the key means of exploring narrative and story-telling.
- To teach children to identify and comment on key features that they see in a variety of media.
- To help children recognise the difference between fact and opinion.
- To give children appropriate opportunities to develop and apply an information technology capability to the study of English.

Learning to read

Most teachers know that when children arrive in reception classes they will be familiar with a whole range of visual information even if they cannot actually read. The ability to read pictures is one of the important building blocks in the making of a young reader. Young children learning to read will scan pictures for visual clues as to the meaning of the written word. However, for children with English as a second language it is not so straightforward. For these children conceptual development happens in their first language and is then transferred into their second language. They will only begin to think in their second language when they are fully bi-lingual, often at a much later stage in their youth. Visual clues are therefore no help if a child cannot comprehend the cultural significance of the illustrations and does not know the word in English. ■

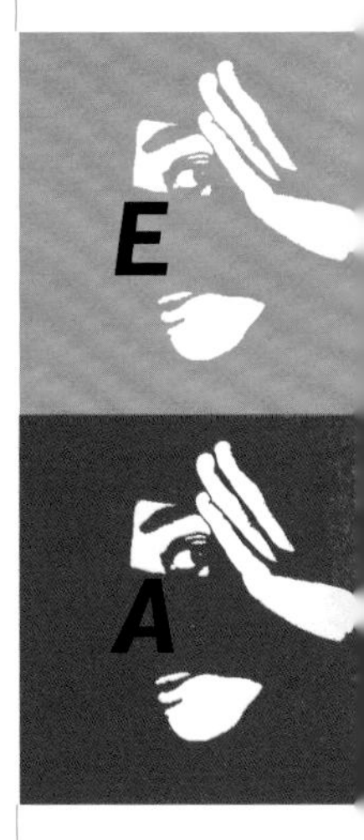

'Picture books'

At Camp JMI School, Hertfordshire, where a large number of children have English as their second language, staff have developed a literacy policy that is applied throughout the school using photography as a central tool for learning.[1] Children take photographs of the school, their home, friends and family which are then coupled with simple texts to make their own reading books. By working with images that are familiar to them the children are stimulated in their learning, the accompanying text is given meaning and they gain access to the written word. Although particularly helpful when teaching children with English as a second language children this approach can be used successfully with any young child learning to read. Using photography in this way with very young children requires time to work on a one to one basis to guide the process and guarantee successful results. You may therefore need to draw on classroom assistants and parents for support. ■

'Picture books' activities

- Ask the children, working in pairs or with an adult, to begin by taking photographs of the classroom and the different areas within it, for example the reading area and the play area. Depending on the resources available they could also photograph other children in the class.

- They should then identify and photograph places around the school. These might include the library, the hall, the office, the staffroom and the playground, in fact anywhere that the children might find themselves during the school day.
- Once the film has been processed a photograph of each area can be stuck into a book and the relevant word to accompany each image written underneath. This could be done by an adult, or, if working with older children, by another child in the class.
- The next stage is for children to take a camera home. Here the support of parents can be drawn on to help the children in their choice of photographs. Again, the results can be put into a book and a parent or an older sister or brother could be asked to write the text to accompany the images. If English is the childrens' or parents' second language the text could be written in both languages. ■

Resources

- 35mm compact camera and colour print film
- Bookmaking materials

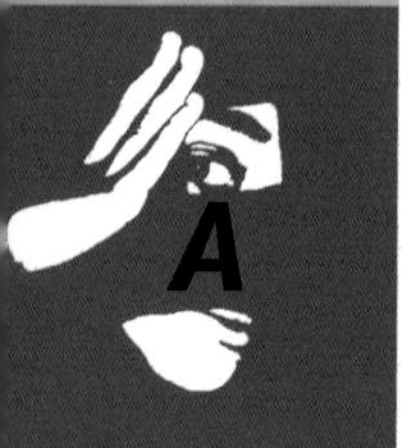

Camp JMI school

Camp JMI school

Story-telling

Pictures and words go hand-in-hand in storybooks and young children will read the illustrations in these books before they can read the text in order to make sense of the story. This can also be the case for children with learning difficulties and the visual medium is an important means of communication. By taking their own photographs and using them to produce their own narratives children who cannot write are given a voice, as visual story-telling acts as another means of communication. ■

English

'Jeremy the Giant'

At Bidwell Brook, Devon, a school for children with moderate and severe learning difficulties, photography is used extensively as a means of creatively delivering the National Curriculum.[2] The project 'Jeremy the Giant' was intended to develop the children's visual and verbal communication skills through the combination of drama, photography and video. The plan was to introduce the activities in an imaginative way.

A class working on the theme of 'Giants' created a seven-feet high puppet that they named Jeremy. Some time later they were told that they had a special mystery visitor, only to discover it was Jeremy, their giant (with a classroom assistant inside). The children's relationship with Jeremy developed over the following weeks and, amongst other activities, they created stories with him, acting them out and recording them with Polaroid and 35mm compact cameras. Photography gave them access to the English curriculum by acting as a vehicle for communication, bypassing what, for some, might have been insurmountable frustrations of conventional literacy. The character of Jeremy provided a vital bridge between reality and the world of the imagination for these children. The project as a whole not only helped to stimulate the children's imagination but also helped to improve their memory and, in a creative way, encouraged animated discussion amongst those with speech and language difficulties.

Clearly the activities that took place at Bidwell Brook were organised to meet particular educational needs. However, there is no reason why elements of this approach should not be taken and adapted to suit your own class. ■

'Jeremy the Giant' activities

- Following the Bidwell Brook model the children could make a giant or a similar character out of old sheets and material. At a later stage the character could magically 'come alive' or one of the children could dress up in the costume and take on the role of that character.
- The experience of seeing this character come to life and the ways in which the class responds to it could be documented with a camera by one of the children. These photographs can then be used in a sequencing activity where the children arrange them in the order that the events took place. They could then rearrange the photographs to create a new sequence that tells a very different story.
- A week after his initial visit the children at Bidwell Brook went in search of Jeremy again and discovered a giant plywood camera and two real cameras loaded with black and white film. Attached to these was a note asking them to produce a photograph album ▸

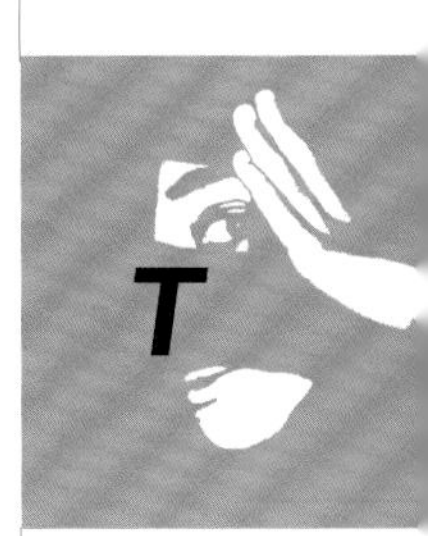

of themselves for Jeremy to keep. This request gave the children a practical reason for taking photographs and for learning to process and print their own images. You could set the children the task of photographing either each other or places around the school in order to build up an album that they could show to a school visitor, or to the imaginary character they have created.

- As the children's relationship with Jeremy developed they involved him in story-based drama activities and used Polaroid cameras to record them. The photographs were then used as a means of recounting these stories immediately. You could ask the class to make up their own scenarios and, working in groups, they could choose one to develop into a dramatic piece. Photographs can then be taken during the performance and used not only as a document and for sequencing activities but to construct new stories by re-ordering the sequence of images. ■

Bidwell Brook School

Bidwell Brook School

Resources

- 35mm camera and colour or black and white film or Polaroid camera and film
- Costume-making materials
- Album or book to compile photographs in

English

‘Witches’

At Greenhead First School, Northumberland, children were introduced to the photographic picture-making process as a source of ideas for story-telling.[3] The class were working on the theme of ‘Journeys’ and, using a camera loaded with black and white film, they took photographs around the school and the immediate locality. These images then provided story-telling material when the children used them in a sequencing exercise, devising a new story of magic and mystery, ghosts and witches from the original photographs. This way of working had an element of spontaneity and unpredictability and the children took to the concept quickly. It encouraged them to focus on the mechanics of story-telling such as point of view, setting the scene, character and speech.

Stories can be translated from one media to another and the children went on to record their still images on to video, adding a voice-over narration. This process allowed them to draft and refine the presentation and organisation of their story, which in turn led to a well-structured narrative. The finished piece was no longer than three minutes and showed the children’s ability to use narrative conventions quite intuitively. It also clearly demonstrated their ability to work imaginatively and creatively with a visual language. ■

Once upon a trime Miranda was turned to stone. Miranda looked like a scarecrow. She looked like a statue.

We were going to find out who had done it.

We fouind a number 10 and a number 9 on the ground.

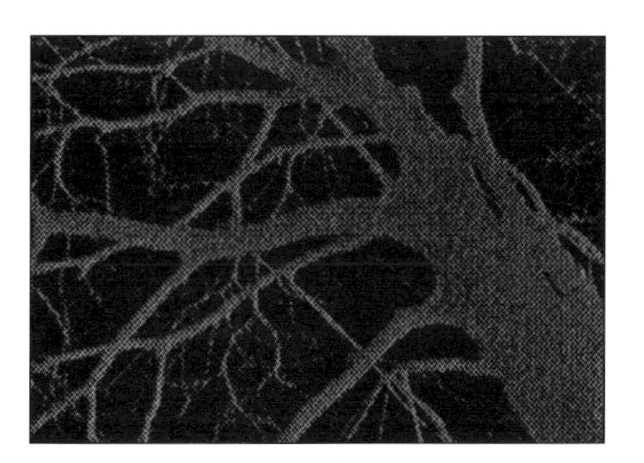

Who’s turned the trees to ice?

Greenhead First School

'Witches' activities

- Having decided on an event, place or activity to focus on, such as a walk around school, divide the class into groups and ask each group to take photographs, using colour or black and white film, of things they notice along the way.
- When the film has been processed ask each group to lay their photographs out on a table and, looking carefully at each one, begin to develop a story from the images. If photographs are taken on a trip or visit that already has some form of narrative sequence the children should create a new sequence to tell a new story.
- Not all of their images need to be used in the sequence and some groups may decide that certain images need to be repeated, in which case photocopies can be used. The children could record their ideas through group discussion, written work or by speaking on audio tape.
- Once a sequence has been decided on the groups should write short captions that tell their story to accompany each image.
- These can then be presented in book form, or, if slide film is used, as a tape/slide with sound and images. Alternatively, some groups may choose to present their work as comic-strip style photostories. ■

Resources

- 35mm camera
- Colour print, black and white or colour slide film
- Tape-recorder if creating tape/slides, or to record ideas
- Video camera and monitor if transferring narratives on to screen

... we found magic spell books.

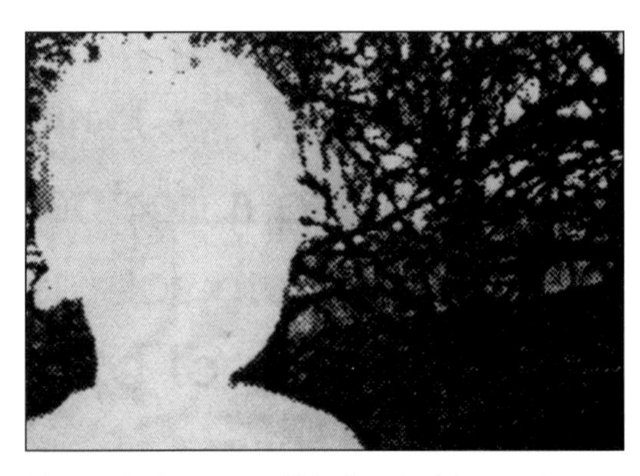

Here is the ice on me. This ghost is giving me the creeps.

We saw a sign that said: Watch out for witches in the west. Watch out for witches and wizards ...

Suddenly ... THE WITCH APPEARED.

Greenhead First School

'Victorian buildings'

A class at West Woodburn First School, Northumberland, produced a photo-narrative for their project work in history that was later re-worked for an activity based in English.[4] The original narrative was produced for the class's project on the Victorians and focused on Victorian buildings in their village. As with the 'Witches' project, the children's still images were copied on to video and a voice-over was added informing the audience about the buildings' construction and history. The same images were then re-used in English at a later date to produce a ghost story. Although made entirely up of the same photographs of buildings, by presenting them in a different order and adding a different voice-over the children managed to create a completely new narrative. The project is a clear example of how photography can be used successfully in cross-curricular work. ■

'Victorian buildings' activities

- To begin this activity you will need a set of photographs that have been created for a different purpose, whether as part of English or another subject, for the children to re-work. Original images could be used, or, if dividing the class into groups, photocopies could be made.
- Ask the children to spread the photographs out on a table and see if any one photograph conjures up particular thoughts or ideas that they could use as a starting point for a story.
- Once their story has a beginning they can begin to develop it with the help of the other images available to them, that is, rather than creating the photographs to tell the story they must create the story from the photographs. ■

West Woodburn First School

'Our school is a Victorian building and here are some more Victorian buildings in our village. Lots of the farm buildings are very old and some of them have been knocked down. **This barn has a stone arch.** Some buildings look Victorian but they aren't.'

Hello, my name is Clare and this is my brother, Billy. This is our new house in West Woodburn. **We like our new village but sometimes we see spooky buildings.** One day, when we were walking home from school we heard a voice from a doorway saying, "I will get you!"'

Resources

- Set of existing photographs, or photographs produced in a different context
- Storyboard sheets to help the children plan (optional)

My story

By taking a camera home to document their lives, children can take photographs that provide an excellent source of material for autobiographical work. Using material that is rich in personal association provides incentives for children to talk and can then build bridges between their own language or dialect, spoken English and the more difficult act of writing. With the focus on their own lives and experiences children may also find it easier to analyse and evaluate their work. A project of this kind can therefore provide a stimulating context in which to deliver many of the requirements of the English curriculum. ■

'Home lives'

At Snowsfields Primary School, London, while working with a photographer in residence, children were given the opportunity to take cameras home.[5] The intention was to reflect the broad cultural mix within the school by showing the children's perceptions of life in a variety of households through their own photographs. The project was also seen as a way of improving children's self-confidence by enabling them to express their sense of themselves, their identities and their linguistic differences through pictures. The images produced formed the basis for autobiographical narratives which, when combined with captions in English and a variety of the children's first languages, were displayed in the school library. These narratives were clearly a direct reflection of the children's lived experience and were popular not only with the children who created them but with children of all ages throughout the school.

When embarking on the project the children were told that their finished work would be presented to an audience who may know all or nothing about them. Therefore when creating captions to accompany their photographs it was important for them to bear this in mind. ■

'Home lives' activities

- Depending on the Key Stage you are working on and how structured you want the project to be, a successful starting point would be to ask the children to plan the photographs they would like to take at home, write accompanying text explaining why the people, places or things they have chosen are significant to them and compile this information in a book. This can then be taken with them when they take the camera home and parents/guardians can refer to it if the children need help or support with the project.

- From the resulting photographs each child should select four to six images that they feel best represent their 'home life'. Through this selection process they should be encouraged to look carefully at each image in terms of content, composition and whether it successfully shows everything they intended it to. In this way they are learning to analyse and evaluate their own work.

'This is my Grandad who lives in Kilburn, he comes to visit every Saturday. My sister Ingrid is looking at him.'

Debbie Evans/Snowsfields Primary School

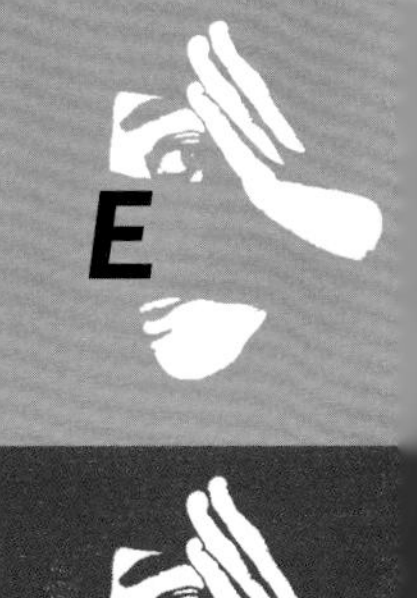

'This is my television in my bedroom. When I am annoyed with my brother, I go and look at it in my bedroom.'

Jay Baxter/Snowsfields Primary School

- Captions or statements should then be written to accompany the selected photographs. At this point there is a tendency for children to write very personally, as though they were writing only for themselves, when they should be thinking about a wider audience. They need to understand that the function of the caption is to place the photograph in context, therefore there may be times when they need to write in greater detail than they had initially planned, or explain the meaning of particular photographs. ■

Resources

- 35mm compact cameras with built-in flash
- Colour or black and white print film

Making stories

Photography has often been used in English as a means of investigating the way in which stories are told. By analysing different kinds of narratives and looking at components such as audience, purpose, genre, scene-setting, story-boarding and presentation children can begin to consider the structure of story-telling. The next step is for children to create their own stories and this involves planning, constructing a narrative, writing captions and editing in a way that is applicable to the particular kind of story that is being told. Children are used to reading visual images, both in their homes and their communities, and respond to image, sound and words in multimedia products through the use of computers at home and in schools. They also live, express, hear and create narratives as part of their everyday lives. There is no reason why all of these resources should not be used in education to provide opportunities for children to develop new texts in a range of forms.

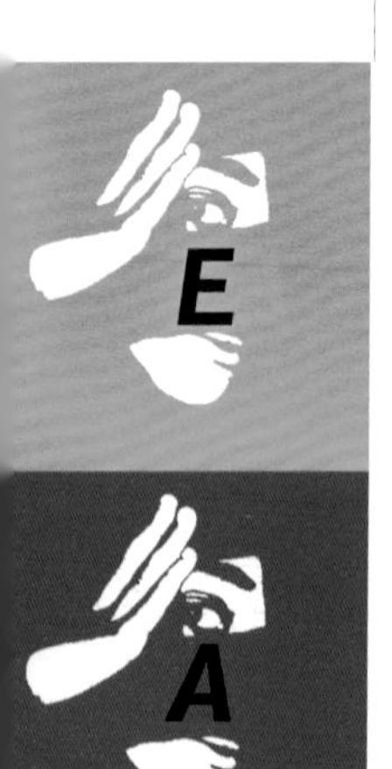

In the revised English Orders, information technology is referred to as a source of information or as a drafting tool. However, interactive multimedia and new developments in digital publishing open up new creative possibilities for children's reading and writing through the production of digital narratives. Children today are competent users of new technologies, due to increasing access to computers in schools and the popularity of home computers – whether used to play games or for educational purposes. They should therefore have the opportunity to engage with computers as a means of production, not just as information and research stations. When constructing digital narratives the same framework applies as for traditional narrative construction, the main difference is that the reader can often choose different pathways through the text, gain further information about certain elements that are highlighted on screen or hear sounds related to the images and, in some cases, add their own pages to be seen by future readers. ■

'Fairy stories'

Using a combination of photographs, drawn illustrations and text a class at Bell Lane First School, Wakefield, created their own fairy stories.[6] As an introduction to the project the children were asked to think of as many fairy story characters as possible, and time was spent, as a class, reading both traditional and non-traditional stories. Working in groups, and following the clear framework shown below, they were then able to develop their own narrative, refine it and produce a finished text in their chosen form. This framework can be used for any narrative project, whether linear or non-linear. ■

'Fairy stories' activities

- Divide the class into groups of five or six and ask the children to decide on the story they want to tell within their groups. The following questions provide a framework for the decisions they will need to make:

a) Audience:	who the story is for? is the audience known or unknown?
b) Purpose:	to tell a story, describe, argue or persuade?
c) Genre:	will it be a thriller, romance, fairytale, etc? traditional or modern?
d) Form:	linear or non-linear narrative? one or a number of endings, that is, branching narrative?
e) Scene-setting:	where will the story be set? what will the characters be like?
f) Storyboarding:	photographs to be taken? how many shots available? portrait of landscape format? will props or costumes be needed? captions, speech bubbles or text?
g) Presentation:	book, tape/slide, branching narrative, comic, etc?

Resources

- 35mm camera and colour print film
- Story books and other narratives for reference
- Paper and drawing materials
- Computer or stencils to generate text

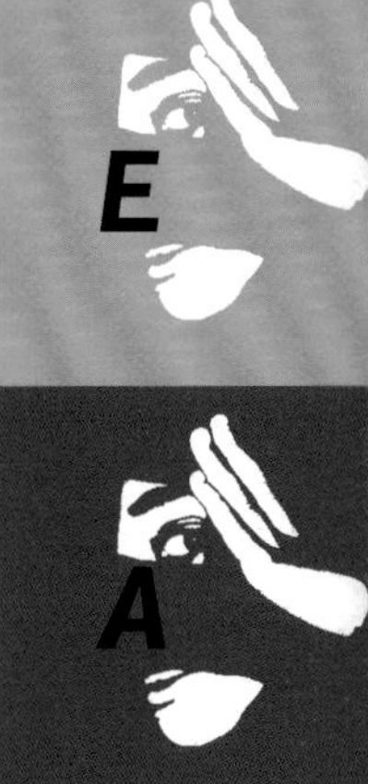

Andrew Burrows, David Forrest, Andrew Varley, Michael and Tom Bell/Bell Lane First School

Andrew Burrows, David Forrest, Andrew Varley, Michael and Tom Bell/Bell Lane First School

- Once the children have considered all of the points above the next stage is for each group member to take on one of the following roles: illustrators, writers, actors, narrators and director.
- All the separate elements of the narrative then need to be worked on and, when finished, brought together and compiled in the chosen form. This may involve decisions as to the scale of photographs and illustrations, editing of text and placing of images within the text. ■

'Escaped chickens'

Children worked on a photostory project at Northgate Middle School, West Sussex, as part of their term's topic on the media.[7] Although undertaken with Key Stage 3 children the approach will work well with children at Key Stage 2 The project was intended to explore the potential for story-telling through the use of photographic images alone, and then through the combination of images and words. As with the previous project children were encouraged to explore narrative devices such as captioning, sequencing and speech bubbles, and to develop their presentation and graphic skills..

Every child in the class was asked to write a story and then, working in groups, they selected one story by a group member and planned their photostory. These were developed with guidelines that could be interpreted by each group according to a different literary, advertising or TV style, for example: thriller, romance, comedy, science-fiction, documentary or news reportage. ■

E

A

'Escaped chickens' activities

- Having organised the class into groups ask each group to plan their storyboards. These should include drawings and notes on the content of each photograph such as the action, camera angle and distance, and the background. The children could also note any captions or speech bubbles they plan to include. These storyboards should then be used as aids when the groups are taking their photographs.

Stuart Tidy, Peter Arthur, Joanne Preece, Mahesh Patel, Kerry Doyle and Gemma Laver/Northgate Middle School

- Each group should then take their photographs. The results could be photocopied to allow the children to make draft layouts of their final photostories.
- Compile a range of examples of existing photostories and comic strips for the class to refer to in terms of page layout and captioning styles. The children should then produce their text in a style to suit the medium, using a computer, handwriting or stencils.
- If the children find that backgrounds or objects they want to use in their photostories are unavailable this can be overcome by using collage to combine their own photographs, images from magazines, or their own drawings. ■

Stuart Tidy, Peter Arthur, Joanne Preece, Mahesh Patel, Kerry Doyle and Gemma Laver/Northgate Middle School

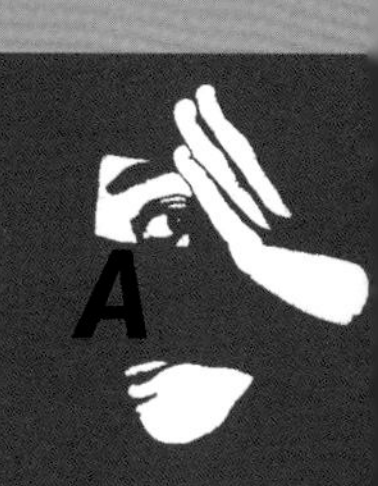

'We had to make a mock-up with some photocopies of the photographs. It wasn't easy to fit everything on but we fitted them on in the end by cropping them. We had to make new captions because the first ones didn't give enough information. ... I think people that have a big sense of humour would like this story. The end result was very good, it caught your eye as well.'

The children

'Planning draft storyboards, taking the photographs and presenting them as photostories strengthened the original stories. This was because the pupils had to struggle to work out how best to use photography, captioning and layout to communicate character, action and mood effectively.'

The teacher

Resources

- Storyboard sheets
- 35mm camera and colour print film
- Existing photostories and comic strips for reference
- Magazines and drawing materials for missing elements
- Computer or stencils to generate text

'Victorian servants – life below stairs'

At Crofton Hammond Junior School, Hampshire, staff and students became involved in the Horizon Project – an initiative in which over forty schools set out to explore how multimedia could enhance children's learning and offer teachers a medium through which they could develop resources to support teaching.[8] Since that time the schools have continued to work with multimedia and are constantly developing their approach to the medium.

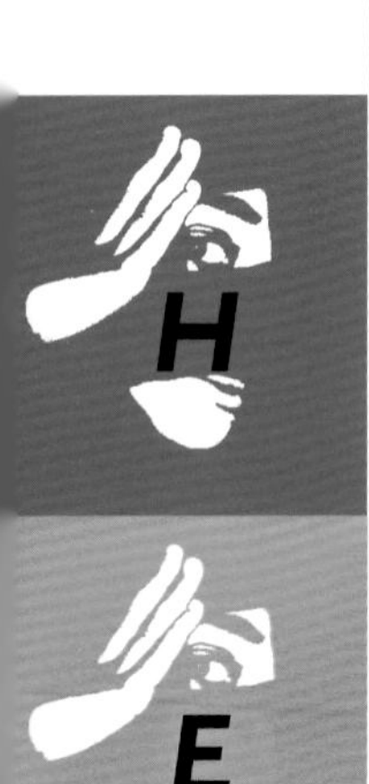

One group of children developed a multimedia project for their topic on the Victorians, but it was two girls in the class who really committed themselves to this way of working. They went on to work independently to create an imaginary 'autobiography', 'Victorian servants – life below stairs', using the software package *Genesis* to create an 'electronic' book. They took on the identity of a cook-housekeeper and a housemaid, and traced the characters' imaginary lives and experiences as they might have been. Working mostly outside school hours they produced some 3,260 words each that they combined with scanned drawings, digital photos taken with a Canon Ion camera, and sound effects to complement the text. The final product illustrates the real potential for multimedia packages to be used as authoring tools in the classroom. For further information on computers and computer software see the technical tips chapter. ■

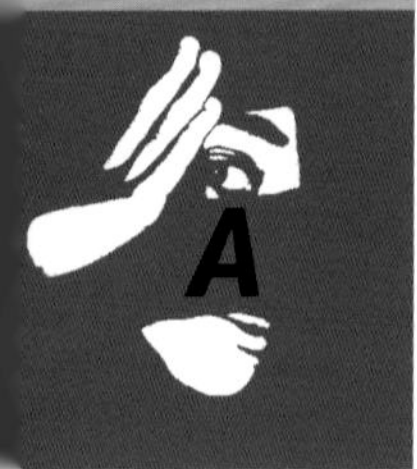

'Victorian servants – life below stairs' activities

- Having selected a theme such as a particular period in the past, or even a period in the future, ask the children to create imaginary autobiographies for themselves that are relevant to the selected theme, using the same framework outlined in the linear narrative projects.
- Having chosen their characters the class will need to be divided into groups and plan title screens for their 'electronic' books. These could include photographs, drawing, text and sound but should act in a similar way to a book cover in that their aim is to encourage the reader to read on.
- The groups should then design their decision page. This will appear after the title page and will offer the user options as to which autobiography they choose to 'read' first and will provide an overall context for their stories. For example, in 'Victorian servants' the decision page read:

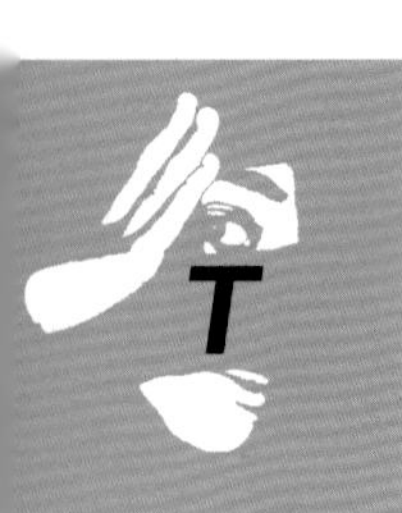

Picture my world

- All wealthy and middle-class Victorian households had servants to cook and clean. They worked long days scrubbing, polishing and tidying. The servants in a wealthy family home might include: a cook and a housemaid.'
- The children could then develop their own characters independently, planning 'pages' to appear on screen that tell of different aspects of their lives or experiences.
- Once all the information has been transferred on to the computer, using a software package such as *Genesis*, the viewer should be able to move around the program at random, moving from one autobiography to another to gain a full picture of what it might be like living in a chosen character's circumstances at that particular point in time. ■

My name is Elizabeth Cudricum, but most people call me Beth.

This is the story of my life.

I have been lucky and have had a good life. Although I have spent most of my life working as a servant for others I have never felt resentful or jealous. That's the way life is meant to be, some people wait and some are waited on !

As you will see as you read my story I started out in the workhouse but ended up as my own mistress, so my story is called

"From Worse to Better"

Emma Foster and Sarah Risden/Crofton Hammond School

Resources

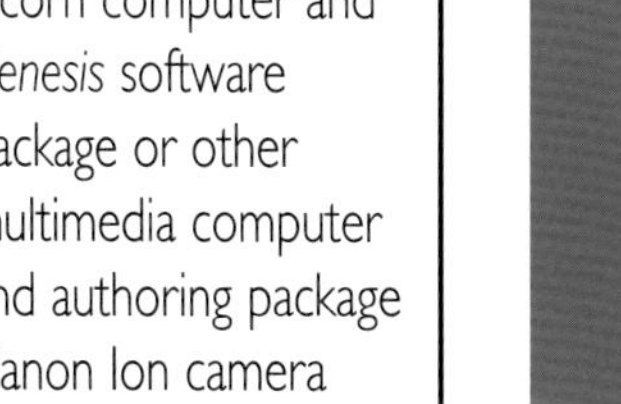
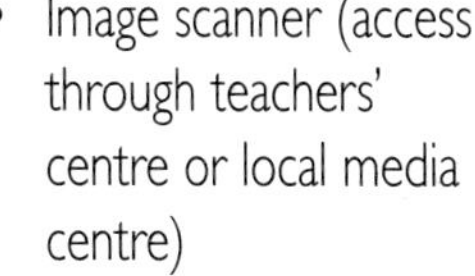

- Acorn computer and *Genesis* software package or other multimedia computer and authoring package
- Canon Ion camera (may be available for loan from local teachers' centre) or 35mm camera and colour print film
- Image scanner (access through teachers' centre or local media centre)

Who tells stories?

All forms of communication employ codes and conventions, in other words, their own grammar, through which meaning is produced. If children are to discuss what they see in a variety of media they will need to develop skills in 'reading' images. Photography provides an accessible starting point for studying the media for two reasons: first, by drawing on existing photographic images in newspapers and magazines children can learn to deconstruct their meaning; and second, through practical production they can apply what they have learnt to control the construction of their own images. By combining these skills they will begin to recognise that different conventions in photography are used in different contexts for different audiences. Through such study children are offered a framework for understanding the diverse ways in which imagery is used in different media forms. ■

'Advertisements'

As an aspect of their topic on the media the class at Northgate Middle School, West Sussex, embarked on a self-image project.[9] Although undertaken with Key Stage 3 children the approach will work well with children at Key Stage 2. The project began with the question: What is the media? and, through class discussion, children identified different media forms including TV, radio, magazines and newspapers. Attention was then focused specifically on advertising and questions were raised as to why people advertise, who advertises, where adverts are consumed and by whom.

Working in pairs the children were asked to look at existing adverts aimed at a broad range of consumers and to identify the target audience. They studied style, content and technique used to sell products including humour and glamour, and discussed whether these adverts exaggerated or distorted 'reality' and if they successfully reached their target audience. The children were then given a brief to create their own advert, using their self-image to sell a product in the same way that celebrities are used to sell particular products.

It is important that time is spent discussing the media in general and teaching children how to read images before embarking on a practical exercise of this kind. The first few activities below give a broad indication of ways this can be done. However, there are many publications available that deal directly with media education and some of these are referenced in the resources section. There are a number of ways of approaching the practical elements of the project – children can either alter existing advertising images by adding their self-portraits, thus personalising them, or gather source material from non-advertising images and combine them with self-portraits and text to change the context and meaning and create their own adverts. ■

'Advertisements' activities

- Collect together a range of photographs of children from a variety of sources such as the family album, school photographs, documentary images and advertisements. Working as a class, and showing one example at a time, ask the children to describe:
  a) what they can see in the photograph (content)
  b) where an image of this kind might be found (context)
  c) the reason they think the photograph was taken (function)
  d) who they think the photograph is taken for (audience)
- Compile the children's answers on the board and place the photographs in categories according to their responses to the questions above.
- You can then ask further questions about the advertising and documentary images in relation to gender, race, class and disability:

a) do the children in these images look like children in the class?
b) who is not shown in these images?
c) are there more images of boys or of girls?
d) are these representations different in any way?

Seeing a large number and range of images together in this way is a clear indication of the ways in which codes and conventions are used in different styles of photography. The images used could be of adults instead of children and the range of images shown could include the wider media such as television adverts, greetings cards, catalogues, film magazines, comics and even computer games.

- The children can then move on to produce their own media image. They need to decide on:

  a) a product that they want to advertise
  b) an appropriate media in which their advert will be placed, for example, newspaper, magazine, brochure or leaflet

  It is a good idea if the children plan their finished image on paper, taking into consideration their position within the image in terms of the scale of their portrait, their body position, etc. and also the text they plan to use.
- Children should then work in pairs to produce a photographic self-portrait. This is best achieved by discussing exactly how they want to be pictured and asking their partner to take the photograph for them.
- These portraits can then be cut out and pasted directly on to their chosen background or, if the scale needs to be altered, photocopies can be made. If applicable, text should then be added to create the finished image. ■

Resources

- Range of advertising and other photographic images
- 35mm camera and colour print film
- Computer to generate text, if applicable
- Photocopier to enlarge/reduce images, if necessary

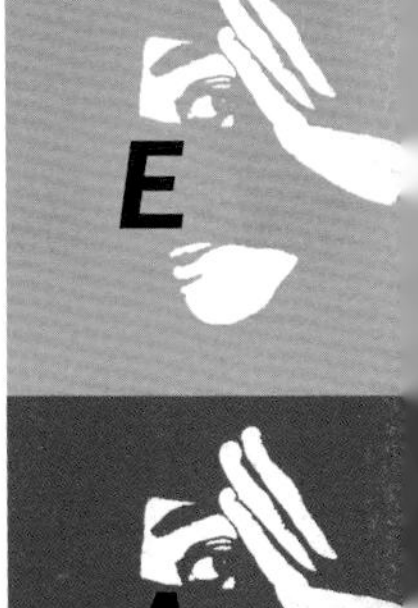

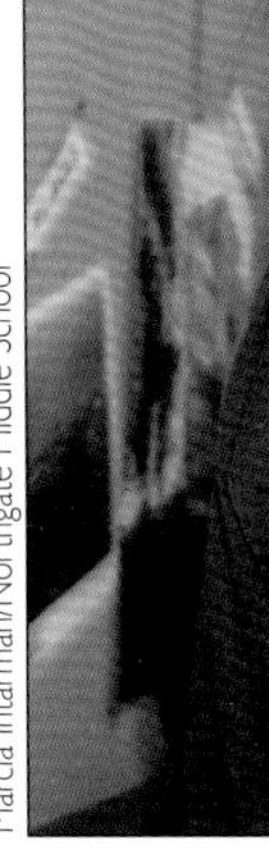
Marcia Intarmah/Northgate Middle School

English

'Newspapers'

In English children are required to read a wide range of information from a variety of sources including newspapers. Whilst newspapers are categorised as non-fiction it is important that children learn to distinguish between fact and opinion. In order to do this they can study the use of photographs in newspapers to understand how meaning is produced and changed through cropping, captioning and contextualisation of these images. By analysing the layout, presentation, tone, style, format and choice of vocabulary, as well as the mix of words and pictures, children can begin to make sense of the structural and organisational features of newspapers and can then create their own newspapers or front pages.

As another strand of their topic, the media, children at Northgate Middle School studied newspaper front pages relating to the Braer oil tanker disaster. The class teacher encouraged them to see the event from different points of view and, working in small groups, they developed their own front pages reporting the incident. The class responded enthusiastically to the task and the project as a whole was successful in raising their awareness of all the issues involved in a single real-life situation. ■

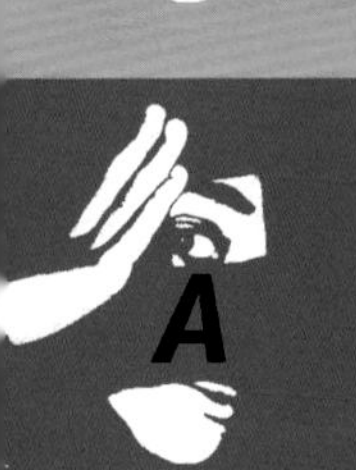

ROYAL EXPRESS 36p

9th January

WAVES OF DEATH

On Tuesday 5th January between 5.30am and 11.23am the Shetland wildlife was at threat by an oil tanker twice the size of the Exxon Valdez called the Braer. The Braer ran aground in North Scotland in the Shetland Islands at Quendale bay. The ship was taking a shortcut to get to Quebec in Canada. One of the engines failed and the ship was stranded in the North Sea. The terrible weather pushed the Braer over to the towering cliffs that easily split the hull of the tanker. Oil gushed out. It is thought about 25 miles of coastline is almost covered in oil. The Braer was carrying 85,000 tonnes of crude oil and is killing the wildlife estimates are over 6,000 birds and seals have died. The effects on the Shetland people would be enormous because of the ruined beaches, air, sea, fisherman and the economy of the Shetland Isle. Theres a huge problem for the farmers because of the contaminated grass which the sheep or vegetables will consume. It is surggested the crew did not warn anyone early enough because there ship would be taken over by salvage. It is also thought that by the the time they did warn someone it was to late and they were nearly already being thrown against the rocks. It was thought to be two hour delay and when they did get there they could only fly a helicopter over the ship to rescue the crew. So there was no one on board who could tie a rope so it could be toed away. Our reporter Jim Smith asked a Shetlander Bill McGimme what he thought of the incident "Well I'm absoulty disgusted! I think it could have been prevented but it wasn't and just look at our wildlife everything is dying but they only care about their money! I've also interviewed Henry Myhm one of the crew. He commented "I couldn't aviod the rocks but I did ring the salvage tug 2.00 hours later.

AT RISK

AT RISK

AT RISK

AT RISK

MILLION BINGO SEE PAGE 2

Northgate Middle School

THE BIG BINGO

THE ECO EXPRESS 20p

FRIDAY 6th JANUARY

SPORTS NEWS

SEE BACK PAGE

SEA SICK

The oil tanker the Braer was sailing from Norway to Quebec when the captain Alexandros Gelis ordered the crew to take a short cut through the Shetland Isles Northen Scotland in a raging storm. Then disaster struck, the engine failed at around 5.30a.m and the storm drifted the tanker towards Guendale Bay. The coast guard ordered an air-sea rescue helicopter to winch the crew to saftey. Then tug boats tried to pull the tanker away from the inland but failed because the crew were not on board. At 11.23a.m The Braer hit rocks and oil was gushing out. The tanker was carrying 22 million gallons of crude oil and it was feared that all 85 thousand tonnes of oil would pour into the sea and would be devastating to the enviroment. Salvage operators could not do anything because of the atrocious weather. Birds, seals, fish and otters have already been washed up on the beach dead. The air is thick with oil and people are being given smog masks. The oil is also mixing with the rain and is killing the grass or contaminating it which is killing the sheep. The economy will be devastated. Marks & Spencer have already said they will not buy salmon from the Shetlanders.

Earlier today Fred Smith who is a fish farmer said "My buisness is ruined and I hope Ultramar America are happy now they have ruined mine and everybody elses life."

AT RISK

Northgate Middle School

'Newspapers' activities

- Collect a number of different newspapers that all include reports about a particular story. If possible these should include local as well as national papers.
- Ask the children, working as a class, if they can identify any differences between the reports in each paper. You could ask the following questions:
  a) do the papers use the same photograph to illustrate the story and, if not, in what way do they differ?
  b) are the headlines or articles written from the same point of view and, if not, how do they differ?
  c) does the story include 'eye witness' accounts in each paper and, if so, are the accounts the same?
- Taking the same event, or choosing a different one, ask the children to work in groups to produce their own front page that reports on the story. If all the groups report the same event it will be possible to ask similar questions of their own finished pieces as were asked of the national and local press.
- Encourage the children to think about the story from a variety of viewpoints to provide different angles and interpretations of the event. With the example of the Braer disaster children were encouraged to see the incident form the position of the islanders, the crew, the ship owners and the World Wildlife Fund. If reporting on a local story the children could conduct their own interviews with the people involved.
- Once they have collected together all the information they need the children should look at the layout of existing front pages before constructing their own. They should focus on the number and width of columns, the number and position of photographs, and the style and placing of headlines and captions.
- Using their own photographs or found images, depending on the event reported, and 'publishing' their text on a computer, the groups must then compile their information to create a finished front page. ■

A

Resources

- Range of newspapers reporting a particular event
- 35mm camera and colour print film or photographs from newspapers or magazines
- Tape-recorder, if children are conducting their own interviews
- Computer to generate text

Project credits

1. 'Picture books': Camp JMI School, Hertfordshire. Key Stages 1 and 2.
   Whole school approach
2. 'Jeremy the Giant': Bidwell Brook Special School, Devon. Key Stages 1 and 2.
   Julia Bond, head of lower school and creative arts, Tim Arnold, media advisory teacher
3. 'Witches': Greenhead First School, Northumberland. Key Stage 1.
   Chris Madge, advisory teacher and Ann Taylor, class teacher
4. 'Victorian buildings': West Woodburn First School, Northumberland. Key Stage 2.
   Chris Madge, advisory teacher and Anne Blades, head teacher
5. 'Home lives': Snowsfields Primary School, London. Key Stages 1 and 2.
   Blackfriars Photography Project, Kamina Walton, photographer and Jasmine Jayham, class teacher
6. 'Fairytales': Bell Lane First School, Wakefield. Key Stage 2.
   Sarah Mumford, advisory teacher, Jenny Cook and Sue Gosidge, class teachers
7. 'Escaped chickens': Northgate Middle School, West Sussex. Key Stage 3.
   Jenny Fox, advisory teacher and Liz Hampson, class teacher
8. 'Victorian servants – life below stairs'': Emma Foster and Sarah Risdon. Crofton Hammond Junior School, Hampshire. Key Stage 2.
   Peter Aitchison and Jenny Wedick, class teachers
9. 'The media – advertisements and newspapers': Northgate Middle School, West Sussex. Key Stage 3.
   Jenny Fox, advisory teacher and Liz Hampson, class teacher ■

Thanks to Mary Fowler for her advice on 'Making stories'.

English planning grid

Key Stage	Project	AT1 Reading	AT2 Speaking and Listening	AT3 Writing
1	Picture books	1ac 2b	1a	
1	Jeremy the Giant		1abd 2a	1abc
1	Witches		1abd	1abc
2	Victorian buildings		1ad 2a	1abc 2ab
1	Home lives		1a	1abc
2	Fairy stories	1ad	1ad	1abc 2ab
2	Escaped chickens	1cd	1a	1abc 2ab
2	Victorian servants – life below stairs		1a	1abc 2ab
2	Advertisements	1a	1a 2ab	1ac 2a
2	Newspapers	1b 2bc	1ad	1abc 2ab

Technical tips

Cameras

The range of cameras available on the market is extensive but the projects documented throughout this book have mostly made use of basic 35mm compact cameras or 35mm SLR cameras. However, certain projects involve the use of pinholes, Polaroid or digital cameras. All of these are explained below.

- **Pinhole camera** – the simplest and cheapest kind of camera, pinholes can be made by children from old shoe boxes, biscuit tins, coffee tins, etc. Instead of using film these cameras involve making an exposure directly on to photographic paper to produce a negative photographic image. There is a step-by-step account outlining how to make a pinhole camera in the science chapter.
- **35mm auto compact camera** – these cameras normally have automatic focusing, a fixed lens and a built-in flash. They range in price from as little as £30 to well over £200, depending on the level of sophistication. Cheaper compacts will normally have a fixed lens with a limited focal length and an automatic flash. For most school use these cameras are quite adequate and there is far less to go wrong with them than with the more expensive electronic compacts. The only drawback is if children want to experiment with close-up photography as the minimum focal range is usually 1.5 metres. Compacts are available with good close-up capabilities but these usually cost quite a lot more. The most important considerations when buying a camera for school are to ensure it has a built-in flash so photographs can be taken indoors and in low light situations, and that the camera itself is sturdy enough to withstand possible knocks and will not fall apart if dropped. Your local camera shop will be able to advise you on the best models depending on the amount you have to spend.
- **35mm SLR (single lens reflex) camera** – these cameras measure light directly through the lens, giving more accurate exposures than many compact cameras. They also have the option of interchangeable lenses, from close-up to wide angle, or as a cheap alternative, screw-on filters that alter the focal length of the lens. A cable release can be attached to the camera enabling children to take their own self-portraits, whereas with a compact they would have to use the self-timer, allowing less control and often leading to unpredictable results. Again, as with the compact, there is a wide and varied range of SLR's on the market which vary greatly in price. It is worth looking in secondhand camera shops as many good SLRs can be found at very low prices.
- **Polaroid camera** – for instant results Polaroid is the obvious choice. Polaroid film generally comes in packs of ten and when a photograph is taken the print is immediately ejected from the front of the camera and the image appears in less than a minute. However, it is the most expensive way of using photography in the classroom and is way beyond most teachers' budgets. With the availability of 1 hour processing it is unlikely that you will need to use this option.
- **Digital camera** – once the photograph has been taken, these cameras can be connected directly into a computer and the images viewed on screen. The advantages over traditional cameras are that images can be taken, viewed and retaken in a very short space of time and there are no film or processing costs. The disadvantages are that the initial outlay for the camera is very high compared to the other options listed, and the image quality is poor in comparison. As outlined in the next section digital cameras are just one way of feeding images into the computer, the other options being considerably cheaper.
- **Disposable cameras** – although in certain situations these can be useful they are an expensive way of taking photographs as they can only be used once, and compared to compact cameras have inferior lenses. The advantage is that there are many different models available, from panoramic to underwater cameras, which could be useful for particular project work. ■

Technical tips

Films

There are two kinds of film you are most likely to use in a classroom situation, depending on the kind of project you are working on.

- 100 ISO (previously known as ASA) colour, or 125 ISO black and white film. This film will give good results if the children are only taking photographs outdoors, or indoors with a flash.
- 400 ISO colour or black and white film. This film should be used if working indoors with available light or other lighting sources such as an anglepoise lamp, as it is better suited to use in low light situations. ■

Computers, video processors and digitisers

Most primary schools have at least one computer and, in many cases, one can be found in every classroom. Although children may regularly use word processing software, paint packages, or view commercial CD-ROMs on these computers, it is still unusual to see them used to manipulate photographic images or to create original multimedia programmes. Projects throughout the book that use computers in this way have been initiated by class teachers and photographers/artists, involving the use of Acorn and Apple Macintosh computers. Photographic, digital and video images have been used and these have been input into the computer in a number of ways which are outlined below.

- **Acorn A3000 series computer** – many schools use Acorn computers and the A3000 series has proved to be popular in primary schools. Two projects in this book used these computers with a digitiser (outlined below) and two others used them with *Genesis* 'authoring' software to produce interactive books. *Genesis* enables children to combine photographic and drawn images with text, sound and graphics to produce multimedia presentations.
- **Apple Macintosh** – these are less commonly used in schools but are used by graphic designers, artists and in advertising. Macintosh computers have been used with *Adobe Photoshop* software in a number of projects in this book. *Photoshop* is simple to use and provides limitless possibilities for image manipulation, from simple cut and paste commands to rendering a lighting effect on an image. Young children have proved to be highly adept at using this software, achieving exciting results. Authoring software is also available for Macintosh, the most popular being *Macromedia Director*.
- **Video processor** – this is, in effect, a simple video camera mounted over a light box which gives you the ability to view colour and black and white negatives and slides on a computer or television screen both as negative and positive images. The processor sends out normal video signals, allowing you to record images onto video tape or, alternatively, if used in conjunction with a digitiser, the images can be viewed on a computer screen and saved on to disk. The projects in this book that made use of this equipment did so purely as a time-saving exercise so that children could take photographs in the morning and view the results in the afternoon. However, processors are not cheap and work out at about the same price as digital cameras.
- **Digitiser** – by linking a digitiser to a computer, still images can be downloaded or grabbed directly from video and converted into image files. The equipment is relatively cheap and allows children to transfer images directly from video on to the computer via the digitiser which can then be printed out on ordinary paper. The advantage of this system is that because of its simplicity children's work can be ideas driven rather than technology driven. ■

Bibliography

For the classroom

As Easy As ABC: a teachers' practical guide. Jasmine Jayham and Kamina Walton, Blackfriars Photography Project 1989. An introduction to photography and language work in the primary classroom. Available from The Photographers' Gallery Bookshop, London. £3.95

Doing things in and about the home – Photographs and activities about work, place and quality. A cultural studies photo-learning pack about the home. Explores and questions stereotypes of role, gender, race. Trentham Books 1983/1987. Available from Trentham Books, tel. 0782 745567. ISBN 0948080 07 8. £4.95

Leaflets available from Lansdowne House Resources Centre, 113 Princess Road East, Leicester. Tel: 0533 551310. £2 each

- *Pinhole Pictures: Making and Using a Pinhole Camera.* Anna Smalley. A teacher's practical 15-page leaflet. ISBN 085 022 2281
- *Capturing Light.* Kim Hames. A 'no darkroom necessary' guide for image making using photographic paper. ISBN 085 022 2575
- *Beyond the Single Frame.* Anna Smalley. ISBN 085 022 2567

What is a family? Photographs and activities about families in Britain. Photography pack. Birmingham DEC 1985. Available from Birmingham Development Education Centre, Gillett Centre, Selly Oak College, Bristol Road, Birmingham B29 6LE. ISBN 0 9506619 5 3. £3

Media Education – Bright Ideas. Avril Harpley. Practical ideas for teachers for activities with children. Includes sections on pinhole photography, photography and storyboarding. 1995. Available from Scholastic Publications Ltd, Marlborough House, Holly Walk, Leamington Spa, Warwickshire, SV32 41.S. ISBN 0 590 76296 6. £6

Photo-Media Studies in a Primary School: Looking through the Family Album. Kim Walden in *Journal of Art and Design Education* Vol 9, No 2, 1990. A theoretical and practical article. Available from NSEAD, The Gatehouse, Corsham Court, Corsham, Wiltshire, SN13 OBZ. Tel: 0249 714925

Picture Stories. Yvonne Davies. An image study pack which builds on the knowledge which children have about visual conventions. Starting points for media education in primary schools pupils. Printed images plus slides and teachers' booklet. BFI 1986. Available from British Film Institute Publications, 21 Stephen Street, London WIP IPL. £12.00 (+£1.25 p&p)

Eye-opener No 1 plus photopack, *Eye-opener No 2* plus photopack. Andrew Bethell. Image analysis and narrative sequencing for pupils to work from. Available from Press Syndicate of the University of Cambridge, The Pitt Building, Trumpington Street, Cambridge CB2 IRP

Every Picture Tells a Story. Martin McCloone with Liam Dwyer and Dermot Stokes. Introductory pack explaining the development of visual literacy skills. Available from the Irish Film Institute, 65 Harcourt Road, Dublin 2. Tel: 010 353 1 679 5744

Available from NATE, 50 Broadfield Road, Broadfield Business Centre, Sheffield S8 0XJ. Prices include p&p.

The Market. Andrew Bethell. An introductory activity involving possible frames from within the scene as if exploring with a film camera. These 'frames' can then be cut out from the image and put into a sequence to show the narrative. English and Media Centre. £3.25

Choosing the News. Michael Simons and Andrew Bethell. A class pack of newspaper stories, alternative headlines and a range of possible photo graphs together with a tabloid layout sheet. English and Media Centre. £8.25

Advertising. Jenny Grahame et al. A4 loose leaf binder and videotape. English and Media Centre 1993. £55

Main Street: Media Education five to seven years. Mary Reid. BFI/Scottish Film Council 1993. ISBN 0 85170 431 X

Classroom Photography: a complete simple guide to making photographs in a classroom. Carol Colledge and Chris Bailey. Teachers' practical guide. Suitable for Key Stages 1 and 2. Ilford UK Sales 1984. Available from Ilford Photo Company, 14-22 Tottenham Street, London WIP OAM. Tel: 0171 636 7890. £10.61

Processing Your First Black and White Film; Making Your First Black and White Print. Two six-page instruction leaflets. Available from Ilford Photo Company, 14-22 Tottenham Street, London WIP OAH. Tel: 0171 636 7890. Free

Practical kits: all available from The Shop, National Museum of Photography, Film and Television, Pictureville, Bradford, BD5 0TR. Cheques to NMSI Trading Ltd.

- *Photograms Kit.* 25 sheets of sun-sensitive paper, one acrylic sheet and instructions. John Adams Toys. £4.95
- *Pinhole Photography Kit.* Camera to make up, developer, fixer, three processing trays, photography paper, safelight cellophane, perspex square, pin, detailed instructions. John Adams Toys. £11.50
- *Take a Closer Look: The big book of optical illusions and activities.* Keith Ray. ISBN 0 9513479 0 X. £3.99
- *Zeotrope Kit.* £1.95
- *Kinetoscope Kit.* £1.95
- *Phenakistoscope Kit.* £1.95

Get the Picture! Developing Visual Literacy in the Infant Classroom. Teachers' practical guide on ways to use photographs to explore representation of people, places, events. Birmingham DEC 1989. Available from Birmingham Development Education Centre, Gillett Centre, Selly Oak Colleges, Bristol Road, Birmingham B29 6LE. ISBN 0 948838094. £5.50

Skills in Sight. Carol Craggs, published by the INSET Project. Video pack including 45 min video, with teachers' notes and stills for Key Stages 2 and 3. Available from The Inset Project, The Retreat, Stanton by Bridge, Derbyshire DE73 IHY. £35

The Mind's Eye. Ian Maley, Alan Duff and Francoise Grellet. Using pictures creatively in language learning. Cambridge University Press 1980. Available from The Photographers' Gallery Bookshop, London. ISBN 0 521 23332 1

Career Aspirations and Gender Issues. Victoria de Rijke and Geoff Cox. This set of posters acts as a visual stimulus to provide discussion and debate about the issues around career aspirations and gender. Accompanied by a leaflet containing teachers' notes and resource list. Middlesex University/Arts Council. Available from Victoria Rijke, Middlesex University, Trent Park, Bramley Road, London N14 4XS. £6

Reading Pictures. BFI Education Department. Introductory pack on Image Studies intended for year 9/10. Image analysis pack. Slides available. Available from BFI Publications, London. £9.50

The Working Camera: the World's First Pop-Up Guide to Photography. John Hedgecoe and Ron Vandermeer. Angus and Robertson

Taking Photos. Lu Jeffrey. A pupils' book. Piccolo

Taking Photographs. A book for pupils. Ladybird 1980

Please note that prices, where given, are offered as a guide. They were correct at the time of going to press, but should be checked prior to ordering

Bibliography

Working Now. A pack for exploring gender roles in the primary classroom. Contains 16 A4 black and white photographs of women in non-traditional work roles, and a teachers' booklet. Birmingham DEC 1989. Available from Birmingham Development Education Centre, Gillett Centre, Selly Oak Colleges, Bristol Road, Birmingham B29 6LE. £5.88 (+£1 p&p)

Disasters in the Classroom. How can teachers approach work on natural disasters without reinforcing the negative images of the 'Third World' presented in the media? Leeds DEC/Oxfam 1989. Available from Oxfam Education Department, 274 Banbury Road, Oxford OX2 7DZ. £3.50 (+£2 p&p)

Images. A pack which examines the way we see the world, through activities on gender roles, racism, wealth and poverty. Photographs and activity cards are also provided. Woodcraft Folk 1987. Available from Woodcraft Folk Supply Department, 13 Ritherdon Road, London SW17 8QE. Tel: 0181 672 6031. £6.00 (+ £1 p&p)

Invisible Workforce. 12 black and white photographs of women working worldwide, illustrating women's contribution to the world economy both in a paid and an unpaid capacity. With fact sheets, pupil activities and teachers' notes. ActionAid 1991. Available from ActionAid, 3 Church Street, Frome, Somerset BA11 IPW. Tel: 0171 281 4101. £5.00

Living and Learning in a Tanzanian Village: A Child's Perspective. Photopack and activities for the primary classroom, using a case study of Kirva Primary School in Tanzania to enable pupils to make links with their own school lives and locality. Manchester DEC 1992. From Manchester Development Education Centre, University of Manchester, 801 Wilmslow Road, Didsbury, Manchester M20 8RC

Photo opportunities. A photopack with an 8-page teachers' booklet and 32 A5 colour photographs (taken from Oxtfam diaries). Oxfam 1991. Available from Oxfam Education Department, 274 Banbury Road, Oxford OX2 7DZ. £6.5 (+£2 p&p)

Moving On. An activity booklet and 20 A4 black and white photographs on Travellers in Britain. Minority Rights Group 1987. Available from Minority Rights Group, 379 Brixton Road, London W9 7DE. Tel: 0171 978 9498. ISBN 0 946690 55 3. £6.95

Selling Pictures. An ideal introduction to the commercial use of images which examines the powerful way in which media representation and stereotypes affect the way in which we define, categorise and evaluate others. British Film Institute 1983. Available from BFI Publications, London. £10.50

Us and the Kids. A set of colour photographs and four booklets designed to encourage parents to talk together about their experiences of bringing up children. Birmingham DEC and Community Education Development Centre 1991. Available from Birmingham Development Education Centre, Gillett Centre, Selly Oak Colleges, Bristol Road, Birmingham B29 6LE. £14.00

Watching the World series. Cathy Nash. Titles include *Investigating Images*; *News from Nicaragua*; *Aspects of Africa*; *Picturing People*; *Whose News?* The series attempts to explore the ways that the media affects our perceptions of the world. Manchester Development Education Project 1988. Available from Manchester Development Education Centre, University of Manchester, 801 Wilmslow Road, Didsbury, Manchester M20 8RG. £6.50 per unit, or £48.00 (+p&p) for all 5 units ■

Sources for teachers

Directory of Media Education Resources. Margaret O'Connor with Dianne Bracken. The Arts Council of Great Britain 1992. Available from AN Publications, PO Box 23, Sunderland, SR4 6DG. Tel: 0191 567 3589. ISBN 0 77287 0651 2. £10.95

Eye to Eye: Using Creativity to Tackle Bullying in Schools. Teacher's pack. £25 +p&p. Send cheque payable to: 'Circle Projects', 76 Main Road, Radcliffe on Trent, Nottingham NG12 2B

Framing the Child: Photography in the Classroom. Watershed Media Centre, Bristol. 32 pages. Full colour. £5.95. ISBN 1 85856 026 8. Distributed by Trentham Books Ltd

The Horizon Project. Illustrated report. CD-ROM and DIY guide to multimedia authoring. £19.99 from Hampshire Microtechnology Centre, Connaught Lane, Paulsgrove, Portsmouth PO6 4SJ

Creating Vision: Photography and the National Curriculum. Sue Isherwood and Nick Stanley. 1993. The Arts Council. ISBN 0 7287 0668 7. Cornerhouse Publications, 70 Oxford Street, Manchester M1 5NH

Close collaborations: art in schools and the wider environment. Norman Binch and Sue Clive. Arts Council of England. £9.95. ISBN 0 7287 0692 X. Distributed by Trentham Books. *Access to Image.* Photo work book. Disability photography issues. VALID, 17–21 Chapel Street, Bradford BD1 5DT

Artists in Schools: a handbook for teachers and artists. Caroline Sharp and Karen Dust. Bedford Square Press. £8.95. ISBN 0 7199 1262 8

Residencies in Education: artists handbook 1. Daniel Dahl and Susan Jones (Ed) 1990. AN Publications. ISBN 0 907730 09 4

National Association for Gallery Education (NAGE) Guides to Gallery Education. Services in the Midlands, North and South West NAGE, 8 Montfort Road, Lewes, East Sussex BN7 1SP. £1.25 each/£3.50 for all three

Photography: towards a multicultural approach. Jim Hornsby. An illustrated 32-page booklet describing a photography in schools project and exploring the links between photography, media education and multicultural education. Includes six accounts of classroom practice. South East Arts with East Sussex County Council 1989. Available from South East Arts. £3

Images of Work: Photography in Art and English. Jim Hornsby. Surrey County Council and South East Arts. 1992. Available from South East Arts. ISBN 0 905593 11 1 £3.50

Photography English and Media Education. Jim Hornsby. South East Arts with East Sussex County Council 1987. Available from South East Arts.

Whose Image? Anti-racist approaches to visual literacy. Edited by Michele Fuirer. Teachers' theoretical and practical reader plus poster. Building Sights/Arts Council 1989. Available from Building Sights, Custard Factory No 1, Gibb Street, Digbeth, Birmingham 9. Tel: 0121 608 7006. ISBN 0 9512956 0 8. £5

Pictures of Health in a Changing World. Jenny Button. Photopack. Available from World Aware, 1 Catton Street, London WC1R 4AB. Tel: 0171 831 3844. £10.95

Children Need Health Care. Edwina Connor. Wayland Press 1988. Available from Wayland Publishers Ltd, 61 Western Road, Hove, East Sussex BN3 1ID. £7.50

Viva! el Peru, Carajo!: the photography and culture of TAFOS. The Photographers' Gallery, London 1991

Bibliography

Portraits and Dreams: Photography and Stories by Children of the Appalachians. Wendy Ewald. Writers and Readers 1985. ISBN 0 86316087 5. £16.95

Magic Eye: Scenes From an Andean Girlhood. Wendy Ewald. Bay Press 1992. ISBN 0 941920 21 6

Common Culture. Paul Willis. Open University Press 1990. ISBN 0 335 09432 7

The Family Album. Sue Isherwood. Broadcasting Support Services. 1988. Available, with cheque payable to 'Channel 4', from Broadcasting Support Services, PO Box 4000, London W3 6XJ. £2.50

The Story of Photography. Michael Langford. Well written and informative book which covers both the history of the photographic process and its many and varied applications. Contains good practical advice with suggested projects and questions. Includes chronology, glossary and brief biographies. Focal Press. ISBN 0 240 51044 5. Paperback, over 180 illustrations, mostly black and white, some colour. £14.96

Practical Photography: MacDonald Guidelines. Margaret Murray, Richard Greenhill and Jo Spence. Available from Macdonald Educational World, Holywell House, Worship Street, London EC2A 2EN

Reading Images. Norfolk TVEI. A book of images with questions asking if images are always what they seem and showing how to read images. Norfolk Educational Press. ISBN 1 8 55260468

Primary Media Education: a curriculum statement. Edited by Cary Bazalgette. BFI/DES National Working Party for Primary Media Education 1989. ISBN 0 85170247 3. *Secondary Media Education: a curriculum statement.* BFI 1991. Edited by Julian Bowker. Accessible and comprehensive guides to the concepts of media education. BFI Education Department, London. ISBN 085170292

Common Culture: Symbolic Work at Play in the Everyday Cultures of the Young. Paul Willis. Open University Press 1990. ISBN 0 335 09431 7. £35

Photography and Visual Education: the report of the Styles and Sites of Photographic Education Research Project. Darren Newbury. Artefact 1993. Available from NSEAD, The Gatehouse, Corsham Court, Corsham, Wiltshire, SN13 0BZ. Tel: 0249 714925 ■

Useful cultural theory

Family Snaps: The Meanings of Domestic Photography. Edited by Jo Spence and Patricia Holland. Virago 1991. Available from Virago Press Limited, 20-23 Mandela Street, Camden Town, London NW1 0HQ. Tel: 0171 383 5150. ISBN 1 85381270 6. £7.99

On Photography. Susan Sontag. A series of general reflections on the development of photography. Penguin. ISBN 0140053972

New Internationalist July 1988 Issue. Article: *Can I Take Your Picture? The Strange World of Photography.* How photographs offer a highly selective view of the world. Highly recommended

Thinking Photography. Edited by Victor Burgin. A challenging collection of essays on photography and cultural theory. Macmillan 1982. ISBN 0 333 27195 S

Art Common Sense and Photography. Camerawork No 3. Article by Victor Burgin

Ways of Seeing. John Berger. Based on television series which explored the ways in which photography took over traditions from painting both in representing property and women and the ways advertisements construct a world. Penguin 1972. ISBN 0563122447

Another Way of Telling. John Berger and Jean Mohr. Granta Books 1989. ISBN 0 14 014006 9. New edition paperback £8.99

Photography and Society. Giselle Freund. Gordon Fraser 1980. ISBN 086092 049 6

Victorian Working Women: Portraits from Life. Michael Hiley. Gordon Fraser 1989. ISBN 0 86092 043 7. £14.99

The Camera Viewed – Writings on 20th Century Photography. Two volumes. Edited by PR Petruck. Datton New York 1979. ISBN 0525 47535 4 and ISBN 0525 47535 2

Pictures on a Page: Photo-journalism, Graphics and Picture. Edited by Harold Evans. Explores the techniques of new photography and photojournalism. Heinemann 1978

Mythologies. Roland Barthes. Cape 1972. New edition. Vintage 1993. ISBN 0 0999 7220 4

Camera Lucida: Reflections on Photography. Roland Barthes. New edition. Vintage 1993. ISBN 0 0999 22541 7. Paperback £5.99

A Short History of Photography. Screen Vol 13 No 1 Spring 1972. Reprinted article by Walter Benjamin

The Work of Art in the Age of Mechanical Reproduction in Illuminations. Reprinted article by Walter Benjamin. Edited by Hannah Arendt. New edition. Fontana 1992. ISBN 0 00 686248 9. £6.99

Seeing Through Photographs. Michael Hiley. Gordon Fraser

Photographic Practices: Towards a Different Image. Edited by Steve Bezencenet and Philip Corrigan. Comedia 1986. ISBN 0 906890 50 0. £9.99

Committing Photography. Su Braden. The Arts Council of Great Britain/Pluto Press 1983. ISBN 0 X6104 701 X. £8.50

About 70 Photographs. Edited by Chris Steele-Perkins. The Arts Council of Great Britain 1980. ISBN 0 7287 02096. £11.95

War Photography: Realism in the Press. John Taylor. Routledge 1991. ISBN 0 415 01064 0. £10.99

Camera Culture. Halla Beloff. Basil Blackwell 1985

The Contest of Meaning: Critical Histories of Photography. Edited by Richard Bolton. MIT Press, Cambridge, Massachusetts. ISBN 0 262 521695. £24.75

The Creatures Time Forgot: Photography and Disability Imagery. David Hevey. Routledge 1992. ISBN 0 415 07019 8. £14.99

In our Own Image: The Coming Revolution in Photography. Fred Ritchin. Aperture 1990. ISBN 0 89 381 399 0. £9.95

Art and Photography. Aaron Scharf. Penguin 1979. New issue. ISBN 0 140 131 329. £14.99

The Burden of Representation: Essays on Photographies and Histories. John Tagg. Macmillan 1988. ISBN 0 333 41823 9. £35. Paperback ISBN 0 333 41824 7. £10.99

Photo Video: Photography in the Age of Computers. Edited by Paul Wombell. Rivers Oram Press 1991. ISBN 1 85489 036 0. £11.95 ■

Networking

National Organisations

The following organisations and individuals are able to offer various forms of support and advice to teachers of photography and media.

AME: Association of Media Education. Jeannette Ayton, Bretton Hall College, West Bretton, Wakefield, West Yorks WF4 4LG. Tel: 0924 830261

Arts Council of England. Vivienne Reiss, visual arts officer, 14 Great Peter Street, London SWIP 3NQ. Tel: 0171 333 0100

British Film Institute. Cary Bazalgette and Julian Bowker, Education Department, 21 Stephen Street, London WIP 1PL. Tel: 0171 255 1444

INIVA: Institute of International Visual Arts. Kirkman House, 12/14 Whitfield Street, London W1P 5RD

INSET Project. Pam Gill, co-ordinator, The Retreat, Stanton by Bridge, Derby DE73 1HY. Tel: 0332 863626

Museum of the Moving Image. Margaret O'Brien, education officer, South Bank Centre, London SE1 8XT. Tel: 0171 928 3535

National Museum of Photography, Film and Television. Amanda Neville, Pictureville, Prince's View, Bradford BD5 0TR. Tel: 0274 725347

National Association for Gallery Education (NAGE). c/o Flick Allen, 8 Montfort Road, Lewes, East Sussex BN7 1SP

National Portrait Gallery. Liz Rideal/Roger Hargreaves, education officers, St. Martin's Place, London WC2H 0HE. Tel: 0171 306 0055

NSEAD: National Society for Education in Art and Design. John Steers, general secretary, The Gatehouse, Corsham Court, Corsham, Wiltshire SN13 0BZ. Tel: 0249 714825

Polaroid UK. Jonathan Robbins, education consultant, The Orchard, Nottington Village, Weymouth, Dorset DT3 4BH. Tel: 0305 812639 ■

Regional Arts Boards

Teachers of photography and media are invited to contact officers of their appropriate Regional Arts Boards (RAB) for advice and information about photography and media resources in their regions and about the RAB's education and training policies.

Eastern Arts Board
Alistair Haines
Cherry Hinton Hall
Cherry Hinton Road
Cambridge CB1 4DW
Tel: 0223 215355

East Midlands Arts
Debbie Hicks
Mountfields House
Forest Road
Loughborough, Leics LE11 3HU
Tel: 0509 218292

London Arts Board
Amanda King
Elme House, 133 Long Acre
London WC2E 9AF
Tel: 0171 240 1313

Northern Arts Board
9–10 Osborne Terrace
Newcastle upon Tyne NE2 1NZ
Tel: 0191 281 6334

North West Arts Board
Tony Woof
12 Harter Street
Manchester M1 6HY
Tel: 0161 228 3062

Southern Arts Board
Hugh Adams
13 St Clement Street
Winchester SO23 9DQ
Tel: 0962 855099

South East Arts Board
Tim Cornish
10 Mount Ephraim
Tunbridge Wells, Kent TN4 8AS
Tel: 0892 515210

South West Arts Board
Sara Fasey
Bradninch Place, Gandy Street
Exeter, Devon EX4 3LS
Tel: 0392 218188

West Midlands Art
Jenny Hayes
82 Granville Street
Birmingham B1 2LH
Tel: 0121 631 3121

Yorkshire and Humberside Arts
Adrian Friedli
21 Bond Street
Dewsbury, W. Yorks WF13 1AX
Tel: 0924 455555

Welsh Arts Council
Holst House
Museum Place
Cardiff CF1 3NX
Tel: 0222 394711

Scottish Arts Council
12 Manor Place
Edinburgh EH3 7DD
Tel: 0131 226 6051

Photography and media centres, galleries and workshops

Below is a selective list of non-commercial photography and media centres, galleries and workshops in England, Scotland and Wales. It is a basic contact list and does not attempt to cover details of access, services and facilities. Listings of privately-run galleries or other arts venues, organisations and contacts may be obtained from the relevant regional arts boards which are listed separately. A good source of information on galleries and exhibition spaces throughout the UK is the *Directory of Exhibition Spaces* published by Artic Producers, (who also publish *Artists Newsletter* and the *Independent Photography Directory*): details of both from PO Box 23, Sunderland, SR4 6DG, tel: 091 567 3589.

Ashbourne, Derbyshire
The Photographers' Place, director, Paul Hill, Bradbourne Ashbourne, Derbyshire DE6 1PB. Tel: 0335 25392

Bath, Avon
f.Stop Gallery and Darkroom, Anna Bush Crewes, education officer, Green Park Station, Bath, Avon BA1 1JB. Tel: 0225 316922

The Royal Photographic Society, Carole Sartain, exhibitions, The Octagon, Milsom Street, Bath, Avon BA1 1DN. Tel: 0225 462841

Batley
Artimedia Centre, director, Brian Cross, 21 Batley Field Hill, Batley, West Yorkshire WF17 0BQ. Tel: 0924 442598

Birmingham
Building Sights, Sue Richardson, co-ordinator, Custard Factory No 1, Gibb Street, Digbeth, Birmingham B9 4AA. Tel: 0121 608 7006

Shooting Stills, manager, Laura Watts, The Custard Factory No 1, Gibb Street, Birmingham B9 4AA. Tel: 0121 603 1300

Midlands Arts Centre, director, Judy Dames, Cannon Hill Park, Edgbaston, Birmingham B12 9QH. Tel: 0121 440 3838

Birmingham Centre for Media Arts (BCMA), director, Nicky Edmunds, 7 Frederick Street, Birmingham B1 3HE.
Tel: 0121 233 4061

Brighton
Lighthouse, Brighton Media Centre, project manager, Jane Finnis, 11 Jew Street, Brighton BN1 1UT. Tel: 0273 202044

Bristol
Barton Hill Photography Project, co-ordinator, Carrie Hitchcock, Bristol Settlement, 43 Dulcie Road, Barton Hill, Bristol BS5 0AK.
Tel: 0272 2556971

Watershed Media Centre, photography co-ordinator, Philippa Goodall, 1 Canons Road, Bristol BS1 5TX. Tel: 0272 276444

Broomfield, Somerset
Photographers at Duckspool, director, Peter Goldfield, Broomfield, Quantock Hills, Somerset TA5 2EG. Tel: 0823 45305

Cambridge
Cambridge Darkroom, director, Peter Ride, Dales Brewery, Gwydir Street, Cambridge CB1 2LJ. Tel: 0223 350725

Cardiff
Ffotogallery, director, Chris Coppock, 31 Charles Street, Cardiff CF1 4EA, Tel: 0222 341667

Media Education Centre, co-ordinator, Cathy Grove, 5 Llandaff Road, Cardiff CF1 9NF. Tel: 0222 396288

Colchester
Signals, co-ordinator, Caroline Norbury, Essex Media Centre, 21 St Peter Street, Colchester CO1 1EW. Tel: 0206 560255

Coventry
Arts Centre, University of Warwick, exhibition organiser, John Gore, Coventry CV4 7AL. Tel: 0203 523060

Derby
Montage Gallery, photography co-ordinator, Elizabeth Ann Williams, 35/36 Queen Street, Derby DE1 3DS. Tel: 0332 295858

The Arbor Darkroom and Gallery, The Arboretum Lodge, Arboretum Square, Derby DE23 8FN. Tel: 0332 291199

Edinburgh
Portfolio Gallery, director, Gloria Chalmers, 43 Candlemaker Row, Edinburgh EH1 2QB. Tel: 0131 220 1910

Stills Gallery, administrator, Lindsay Lewis, 105 High Street, Edinburgh EH1 1TB. Tel: 0131 557 1140

Exeter
Exeter Darkroom, co-ordinator, Martin Hampton, Exeter and Devon Arts Centre, Gandy Street, Exeter EX4 3LS. Tel: 0392 432617

Exmoor
Exmoor Photographers Gallery, Peter Hounslow, 39 High Street, 39 High Street, Dulverton, Somerset TA22 9DW. Tel: 0398 23286

Glasgow
Street Level, exhibition and education officers, Catriona Grant and Martha McCulloch, 279-281 High Street, Glasgow G4 0QS.
Tel: 041 552 2151

Kendal
Brewery Arts Centre, Hugh Greenland, Highgate, Kendal, Cumbria LA9 4HE. Tel: 0539 25133

Lancaster
Dukes Cinema, Tim Webb, Moor Lane, Lancaster LA1 1QE.
Tel: 0524 67461

Leeds
Matrix – Women's Photography Archive, Val Green, 47 Sandhurst Terrace, Leeds LS7 4NZ. Tel: 0532 496407

Pavilion – Women's Photography Centre, 2 Woodhouse Square, Leeds LS3 1AD. Tel: 0532 453329

Leicester
Picture House Gallery and Media Education Centre, photography and education worker, Anna Smalley, 113 Princess Road East, Leicester LE1 7LA. Tel: 0533 549083

Liverpool
Open Eye Gallery, photography organiser, Dave Williams, 110-112 Bold Street, Liverpool L1 4HY. Tel: 0151 708 5699

051 Media Centre, 1 Mouth Pleasant, Liverpool L3 5SX.
Tel: 0151 707 0257

Black Witch, Training and Photography Exhibition, Trading Places, Holmes Building, 46 Wood Street, Liverpool L1 4AH

Networking

London

Association of Photographers, exhibitions and education officer, Jackie Kelley, 9-10 Domingo Street, London EC1Y 0TA. Tel: 0171 608 1441

Art of Change (previously Docklands Community Poster Project) co-ordinator, Peter Dunn, Level 3, Lion Court, 435 The Highway, Wapping, London E1 9HT. Tel: 0171 702 8802

Artec, director, Frank Boyd, 393-395 City Road, London EC1V 1NE. Tel: 0171 833 1875

Autograph, director, Mark Sealy, 13-16 Vine Hill, London EC1R 5DX. Tel: 0171 278 2333

Blackfriars Photography Project, 177 Abbey Street, London SE1. Tel: 0171 237 9312

Camerawork, director, Barbara Hunt, 121 Roman Road, Bethnal Green, London E2 0QN. Tel: 0181 980 6256

Hamiltons Gallery, Sascha Hackel or Patrizia Saro, 13 Carlos Place, London W1. Tel: 0171 499 9494

Monocrone Women's Photography Collective, Sophie Fuller, Clapham Pool, Clapham Manor Street, London SW4 6DB. Tel: 0171 926 0703

North Paddington Community Darkroom, Maria Pedro, YAA Asantewa Arts Centre, 1 Chippenham Mews, Maida Village, London W9 2A., Tel: 0171 286 5543

Paddington Printshop, John Phillips, Basement, 1 Elgin Avenue, London W9 3PR. Tel: 0171 286 1123

Photofusion, Alistair Raphael, 17a Electric Lane, Brixton, London SW9 8LA. Tel: 0171 738 5774

The Photographers' Gallery, director, Paul Wombell, 5 and 8 Great Newport Street, London WC2H 7HY, Tel: 0171 831 1772

Portfolio Gallery, Nicky Akehurst, 345 Portobello Road, London W10 5SA. Tel: 0181 960 0453

Special Photographers' Gallery, exhibition organiser, Catherine Turner, 21 Kensington Park Road, London W11 2EU. Tel: 0171 221 3489

TIPP (Independent Photography Project), Rothbury Hall, Azof Street, Greenwich, London SE10 0EF

Zelda Cheatle Gallery, director, Zelda Cheatle, 8 Cecil Court, London WC2N 4HE. Tel: 0171 836 0506

Maidstone

Cross Channel Photographic Mission, c/o County Hall, Maidstone ME4 1XQ. Tel: 0622 694457

Manchester

Cornerhouse, Stephen Snoddy, exhibitions organiser, 70 Oxford Street, Manchester M1 5NH. Tel: 0161 228 7621

Counter Image, director, Tony Clancy, 3rd Floor, Fraser House, 36 Charlotte Street, Manchester M1 4FD. Tel: 0161 228 3551

Workers Film Association Media and Cultural Centre, Wowo Wauters, 9 Lucy Street, Manchester M15 4BX. Tel: 0161 848 9782

Newcastle

Zone Gallery, directors, Kate Tregaskis and David Sinden, 8 Westgate Road, Newcastle upon Tyne NE1 1SG. Tel: 0191 232 8833

Side Gallery, director, Richard Grassick, 9 Side, Newcastle upon Tyne NE1 3JE. Tel: 0191 232 2000

Norwich

Norwich Arts Centre, Peter Kent, Reeves Yard, St Benedicts Street, Norwich NR2 4PG. Tel: 0603 660352

Nottingham

Focal Point Photographers, Michael Hopkinson or Laurence McDowall, Castle House, 2 Castle Boulevard, Nottingham NG7 1FB. Tel: 0602 588876

Oxford

Oxford Photography, Jacqui Mansfield, c/o Department of Visual Arts, Oxford Brookes University, Gipsy Lane, Headington, Oxford OX3 0B. Tel: 0865 819477

Photographers Workshop, Keith Barnes, 103 104 St Mary's Road. Cowley, Oxford OX4 1QD. Tel: 0733 237073

Salford

Viewpoint Photography Gallery, photography officer, Graham Marsden, The Old Fire Station, The Crescent, Salford M5 4NZ, Tel: 061 737 1040

Sheffield

Untitled Gallery, director, Carol Maund, 1 Brown Street, Sheffield S1 2BS. Tel: 0742 725947

Southampton

Mount Pleasant Photography Workshop, Martin Reid, c/o Mount Pleasant Middle School, Mount Pleasant Road, Southampton. Tel: 0703 231977

Southend

Focal Point Gallery, director, Ronnie Simpson, Central Library, Victoria Avenue, Southend on Sea, Essex SS2 6EX. Tel: 0702 612621

Stockton, Cleveland

Dovecot Arts Centre, film and photography officer, Paul Mellor, Dovecot Street, Stockton, Cleveland. Tel: 0642 611625

Swindon

Media Arts, media arts manager, Carol Comley, Town Hall Studios, Regent Circus, Swindon SN1 1QF. Tel: 0793 526161 ext. 3450

West Bromwich

Jubilee Arts, director, Sylvia King, 84 High Street, West Bromwich, West Midlands B70 8HP. Tel: 0121 553 6862

Wolverhampton

The Lighthouse Media Centre, exhibition organiser, Evelyn Wilson, Chubb House, Friar Street, Wolverhampton WV1 1HT. Tel: 0902 716044

York

Impressions Gallery, director, Cheryl Reynolds, 29 Castlegate, Castlewalk, York YO1 1RN. Tel: 0904 654724 ■